D1200303

WORLD WAR II
PACIFIC
CHRONICLE OF AMERICA'S WARS

Barbara Williams

LERNER PUBLICATIONS COMPANY

MINNEAPOLIS

Lerner Publications Company
A division of Lerner Publishing Group
241 First Avenue North
Minneapolis, MN 55401

Website address: www.lernerbooks.com

Library of Congress Cataloging-in-Publication Data

Williams, Barbara.
  World War II. Pacific / by Barbara Williams.
    p.   cm. — (Chronicle of America's wars)
  Includes bibliographical references and index.
  ISBN: 0–8225–0138–4 (lib. bdg.)
    1. World War, 1939–1945—Pacific Area. 2. World War, 1939–1945—Campaigns—Pacific Area. 3. World War, 1939–1945—United States. I. Title: Pacific. II. Title: World War Two. III. Title: World War 2. IV. Title. V. Series.
  D767.A66 2005
  940.54'26-dc22   2004003371

Manufactured in the United States of America
1 2 3 4 5 6 – JR – 10 09 08 07 06 05

TABLE OF CONTENTS

AUTHOR ACKNOWLEDGMENTS

Many of the quotes in this book came from uncopyrighted material I personally received from veterans of World War II or from their surviving relatives. I am grateful to them all.

For Chapter 4, I relied heavily on *The Spirit of the "Sammy B,"* by Robert W. Copeland and Jack E. O'Neill. Everett "Bob" Roberts Jr., who served as executive officer of USS *Roberts,* shared a copy of his lengthy memoir, and I have communicated at length with other survivors, who were of inestimable help. They include Thomas J. Stevenson Jr., J. Dudley Moylan, Vincent N. Goodrich, Robert M. Harden, James E. Patterson, Adolph Herrera, Louis A. Gould, Sam Blue, George Bray, Donald Young, Jack Yusen, and Richard Rohde. My dear friend Leah B. Felt is the widow of still another *Roberts* survivor, H. Whitney Felt. It was Whit who first introduced me to the story of his ship. After his death, Leah gave me the memoir that Whit had left on his computer before his death in 1998.

Paul Cracroft, another good friend, shared a vastly different kind of memoir that his deceased older brother had recorded. A popular MC and humorous speaker, Lawrence Cracroft managed a tongue-in-cheek spin on the grim Pacific battles that he fought in as a marine captain. Other relatives of deceased World War II veterans, including Suzanne Hartley, daughter of Robert Copeland, and Margaret Blemis, sister of Jack Moore, provided me with valuable unpublished memoirs. Old friends who participated in Pacific Theater battles and shared their incisive recollections include Gordon Douglass, Richard L. Gunn, Clyde E. Weeks Jr., and Nad A. Peterson. They not only shared their personal records but also answered my endless questions by telephone and e-mail. A neighbor, H. Michael Moss, recounted fascinating anecdotes about his service as a Japanese language expert on the island of Saipan. When I exhausted all the veterans I knew, I turned to nonmilitary friends, including Naomi Barnett, Dorothy Fry, Bonnie Robinson, Kevin Peterson, Helen Warnock, Vivian Olsen, Elaine Brockbank, and Lily Havey. They, in turn, led me to a host of their own helpful relatives and friends. Among those referrals were Adeline and Gerson Reisler; John, Coral, and Debbie Clifford; Kenneth J. O'Leary and Erin O'Leary-Jepsen; Carl J. Schlegel; William H. Fotheringham; Earl G. Hoyt; Stephen Stanford; Henry F. Brookers; Fred Adrian; Harvey Gittler; Warren Wickes; Charles Matthews; and Hugh McCorkle. Especially helpful was the lengthy memoir, "King One: Service in the United States Marine Corps in World War II," by Jeptha Carrell, a former captain and veteran of Guadalcanal. Carrell not only writes with exceptional wisdom and clarity, but his bound manuscript contains interesting photographs and sketches. Another friend, Nicholas G.

Smith, generously let me borrow videos from his personal library. Several veterans were kind enough to read portions of my manuscript and provide suggestions. They include Carl Schlegel, Richard Rohde, Dudley Moylan, Vincent Goodrich, Thomas Stevenson, and Jack Yusen. Above all, I am grateful to my husband, J. D. Williams, who volunteered to read my entire manuscript. Furthermore, he encouraged me through every step of the writing and even refereed my warfare with a computer that stubbornly resisted the commands I tried to give it. Most importantly, his patience and encouragement remained steady through weeks of his duty as chef, bed maker, and chauffeur as I recuperated from surgery and struggled with a violent and never-ending case of hives. I love him very much.

INTRODUCTION

December 7, 1941, began as a balmy Sunday on the Hawaiian island of Oahu. The island was home to the U.S. naval base at Pearl Harbor, headquarters of the U.S. Navy's Pacific Fleet. On that December morning, most servicemen at the base were enjoying a day off. Some were writing letters to their wives or girlfriends back home. Some were preparing for a baseball game on a pier near the harbor. Others were returning to their ships after a night on the town. Still more in dress white uniforms were clustered on the beach waiting for an outdoor church service.

Then, shortly before 8:00 A.M., scores of planes droned toward Oahu from three directions. Some servicemen noticed the planes, but most paid little attention. Assuming the aircraft were U.S. B-17s returning to nearby Hickam Field, the men below continued on with what they had been doing.

But the planes, with bright red circles on their wings and sides, were not American. And they were flying straight toward Ford Island in the center of Pearl Harbor.

On a hilltop overlooking the harbor, the small son of a navy officer noticed the pretty red circles on the closest planes. He wondered why the planes did not have the familiar white stars on blue circles that were normally painted on U.S. aircraft. Did the new designs indicate some kind of military exercise no one had told him about?

Unaware, he chased after the planes, laughing and waving.

Seeing her son through an open doorway, the boy's mother shrieked for him to come inside. She knew what the red circles meant—the planes were Japanese.

THE WORLD AT WAR

By December 1941, the world was at war. Germany, under the leadership of dictator Adolf Hitler, had already conquered most of its neighbors in Europe. Italy, a German ally, had attacked parts of North Africa. The only European nations able to resist the German and Italian aggressors were Great Britain to the west and the Soviet Union to the east. Those nations were engaged in desperate land, air, and sea battles against German and Italian armies.

At the same time, Japan wanted to control Asia and the islands of the Pacific Ocean. Within their densely populated island nation, the Japanese couldn't produce all the goods they needed for modern, industrial life, especially oil. In a quest for more territory and resources, Japan seized parts of China in 1931 and 1937. In 1940 and 1941, Japan took over much of Southeast Asia.

Italy and Germany had formed an alliance in the 1930s, agreeing to back one another's military efforts. In 1940 Japan joined the alliance. The three countries became known as the Axis powers. The nations fighting the Axis—led by Great Britain, the Soviet Union, and China—were named the Allies. The near-global conflict, which began after Germany invaded Poland in 1939, was called World War II.

For two years, the United States did not join in the fighting. But it did support the Allies by sending weapons, food, and other supplies to Allied armies in Europe. Most Americans were alarmed by Hitler's march across Europe. U.S. citizens had many ties to Europe, including a common heritage. They wanted to help the nations fighting Hitler and his Nazis.

ROOSEVELT AND ISOLATIONISM

In 1939 most Americans, including many members of Congress, held an isolationist attitude. After World War I, they strongly opposed fighting another war abroad. But President Roosevelt knew that Britain couldn't defeat the Axis powers without help.

FAST FACT

FROM BAD TO WORSE

Few Americans worried about Japanese aggression in Asia, however. Ordinary citizens were unfamiliar with the political situation in faraway Japan. But U.S. leaders knew what most citizens did not—that U.S.-Japanese relations had been deteriorating for many years.

Shortly after World War I (1914–1918), Japan signed a treaty with the United States, Great Britain, and France. Japanese leaders were angry with the agreement, which limited the size of their navy. But Japan signed the agreement under pressure from the three more powerful nations. Secretly, the Japanese continued to build naval ships. In 1924 the U.S. Congress passed an immigration act, denying Japanese citizens the right to move to the United States. In Japan this law created additional anger against the United States.

Japan invaded Manchuria, a region of China, in 1931. The United States sided with China. In response to the invasion, the United States stopped selling Japan petroleum (oil) products, machine tools, steel, and other materials that could be used to make weapons. The Japanese reacted by cutting off trade with the United States.

In 1932 a small group of Japanese military leaders assassinated the Japanese prime minister and took control of the government. In theory, a young emperor named Hirohito (said to be descended from the Shinto sun goddess) ruled Japan. In reality, military leaders, called the Japanese High Command, actually controlled the nation.

Japanese forces push into China during the Japanese invasion of that country in the late 1930s. With success in China, the Japanese government set its sights on conquest of all of Asia.

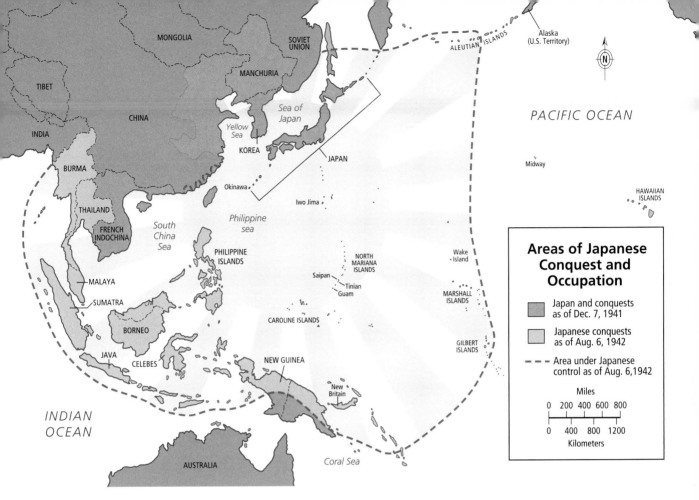

In 1940 Japan allied itself with Germany and Italy, becoming a member of the Axis powers. It also released a document called "The Greater East Asia Co-Prosperity Sphere." This declaration stated the Japanese right to control all of Asia and the islands of the Pacific Ocean. By 1941 Japan had conquered large portions of China and Southeast Asia. It stood poised to take over the rest of Asia. But first, it would have to subdue a nation with a strong navy and air force based in the Pacific: the United States of America.

SNEAK ATTACK

One Japanese leader was uncertain about a war with the United States. Admiral Isoroku Yamamoto had studied at Harvard University in Massachusetts and had served as a diplomat in Washington, D.C. As a result, he had respect for U.S. industry. He knew that in a lengthy war, the United States was likely to win. But in 1941, Japan's navy and air force were far superior to those of the United States. Yamamoto felt that Japan needed to keep the war with the United States brief by scoring a big victory early.

So the Japanese planned a surprise attack. On the morning of December 7, 1941, a fleet of 33 Japanese ships sneaked into position about 230 miles north of Oahu. From there, more than 350 planes took off from the decks of aircraft carriers (also called flattops because of their flat flight decks) and sped toward Pearl Harbor.

THE JAPANESE POINT OF VIEW

After World War I (1914–1918), economic depression spread to nations throughout the globe, including Japan. Sales dropped sharply for Japanese canned fish, silks, linens, bamboo furnishings, and other products. Japan's export trade, which had flourished before the war, withered and died. Businesses closed, and people lost their jobs.

At the same time, the Japanese people needed imports to survive. The island nation couldn't produce enough rice, its main food, to feed its population. Japan needed more land. It needed more steel, rubber, and petroleum to make modern machines.

Japanese military leaders began looking for resources in other parts of Asia. They were particularly interested in the Manchuria region of China. This area not only had many natural resources but also had vast areas of land and excellent ports for shipping.

Believing their emperor was descended from the sun goddess, Japanese commanders argued that they had a divine (god-given) right to seize countries that possessed the resources they needed. On September 18, 1931, Japan

Prime Minister Hideki Tojo addresses Japanese officials on the need for war in the early 1940s.

sent troops into Manchuria. An international peacekeeping organization called the League of Nations, which Japan had joined after World War I, condemned the Japanese invasion. But the League of Nations lacked the power to stop Japan. The United States sided with China and stopped selling oil and machine tools to Japan.

Angry at the United States but pleased by the easy takeover of Manchuria, Japanese military leaders dug mines and built factories there. Growing more confident, they assassinated the Japanese prime minister and other liberal politicians. With General Hideki Tojo as their spokesman, they began preparing to take over other parts of Asia and the islands of the Pacific Ocean. But they feared that the powerful U.S. Army and U.S. Navy might stand in their way.

The Japanese believed they had the Shinto gods on their side (Shinto is an ancient Japanese religion). They also believed in the code of Bushido (the way of the warrior). Most Japanese soldiers, especially volunteers, still honored this ancient code. Bushido placed loyalty to leaders above wealth—even above the warrior's own life. According to Bushido, the side in warfare that demonstrated the strongest faith, rather than the best technology, would ultimately succeed. Faith was demonstrated by the sacrifice of self and an absolute refusal to surrender. To enforce that ideal, General Tojo established a rule that seemed incredible by Western standards. Any man who escaped his captors after being taken prisoner would be executed in disgrace by his own regiment.

In 1940 Tojo became Japan's minister of war. In October 1941, he became prime minister. As prime minister, he bombarded his people with anti-American propaganda (messages spread to further a political cause). He claimed that the United States was trying to dominate the world and convinced Japanese citizens to pledge all their energies to defeating the United States. Civilians were so happy about the sneak attack on Pearl Harbor that they greeted returning pilots with a wild victory parade in Tokyo.

"REMEMBER PEARL HARBOR"

1

At 7:55 A.M., the peaceful Sunday morning on Oahu turned to horror. The wave of planes that swept in from the ocean suddenly began to dive. Bombs wailed and exploded. American sirens blared, and servicemen ran frantically through black smoke toward battle stations on their ships.

Within the first few minutes of the attack, the battleship *Arizona,* lined up with a group of other huge ships in Battleship Row, exploded and sank. One witness said the sky above the ship seemed to be raining men. More than 1,000 of its crew members were killed by the explosion or drowned inside the ship. The battleship *West Virginia* also sank, and *Oklahoma* rolled onto its side.

Pounding by the first wave of Japanese planes continued for 30 minutes. Then, after a 15-minute lull, another wave of planes swept into the harbor, attacking for an hour. The second wave lacked the advantage of surprise, and a few Americans were able to send up antiaircraft fire.

Did You Know?

In 1941 the United States broke several Japanese codes, revealing hints of Japanese military plans to U.S. intelligence. Some historians believe that President Roosevelt was told about a possible attack on Pearl Harbor. These historians argue that he let it occur to rile up U.S. hatred for the Axis.

By then the flames and smoke from the first assault also made it difficult for the Japanese pilots to see, but the second wave still caused much damage.

"Tora! Tora! Tora!" commander Mitsuo Fuchida of the Japanese Imperial Navy radioed to his commanders with the Japanese fleet. That message (meaning "Tiger! Tiger! Tiger!") was a prearranged signal to announce that the attack had taken the Americans by total surprise.

As U.S. generals and admirals assessed the damage, it seemed that the Japanese had scored an enormous victory at Pearl Harbor. Luckily, all U.S. aircraft carriers and their planes had been out at sea that day, but eight battleships, three cruisers, three destroyers, and eight other vessels had been sunk or severely crippled. The attack had destroyed approximately one-third of the military planes near Pearl Harbor. More than 2,300 Americans had been killed, and about 2,000 had been wounded.

THE UNITED STATES GOES TO WAR

Addressing the U.S. Congress the day after the Japanese attack, President Franklin Delano Roosevelt called December 7, 1941, "A date which will live in infamy [a state of evil]." In addition to Pearl Harbor, Japanese forces had attacked other sites in the Pacific within a 24-hour period. Roosevelt went on to list them:

EYEWITNESS QUOTE: PEARL HARBOR

"There was a big long sheet of very black smoke out in the bay. As I ran to the officers' Boat Landing, I heard one sailor holler to another that . . . the *Oklahoma* was sunk. My heart sank with the ship. I was supposed to be on board with about 80 men in my division. . . . In my mind's eye I could see them floundering below."

—Gordon E. Douglass, U.S. Navy

Yesterday, the Japanese government also launched an attack against Malaya.

Last night, Japanese forces attacked Hong Kong.

Last night, Japanese forces attacked Guam.

Last night, Japanese forces attacked the Philippine Islands.

Last night, the Japanese attacked Wake Island.

This morning, the Japanese attacked Midway Island.

Japan has, therefore, undertaken a surprise offensive extending throughout the Pacific area.

The sneak attack had occurred before an official declaration of war. And it came at a time when U.S. and Japanese diplomats in Washington, D.C., had been peacefully trying to negotiate their countries' differences.

Congress responded to President Roosevelt's address by declaring war on Japan. Then, because Japan had signed a pact (agreement) with Germany and Italy, those two countries declared war on the United States. The United States was suddenly thrust into World War II in two areas—Europe and the Pacific Ocean.

Americans' readiness for war was no match for that of the Japanese. The United States had less than half as many ships and aircraft as

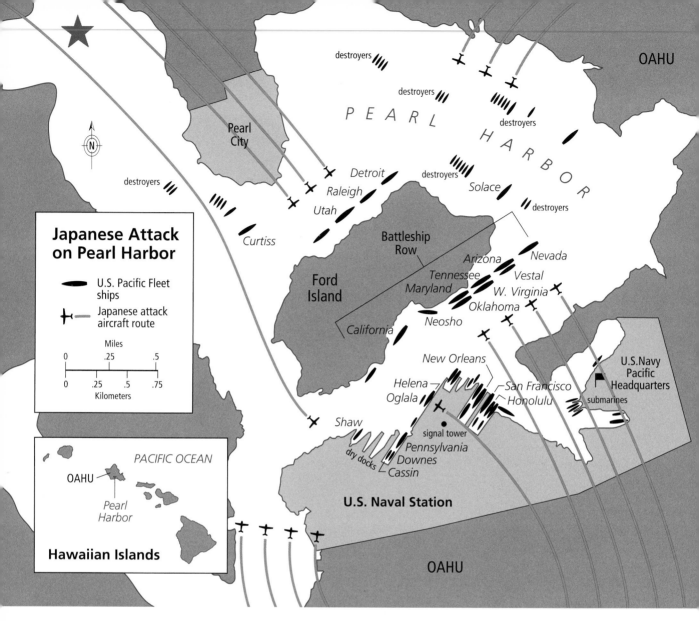

Japanese Attack on Pearl Harbor

U.S. Pacific Fleet ships

Japanese attack aircraft route

Miles
0   .25   .5

0   .25   .5   .75
Kilometers

PACIFIC OCEAN

OAHU

Pearl Harbor

Hawaiian Islands

OAHU

destroyers

destroyers

destroyers

P E A R L

H A R B O R

destroyers

Detroit

Raleigh

Utah

destroyers

Solace

destroyers

Curtiss

Battleship Row

Ford Island

Nevada

Arizona

Tennessee

Vestal

Maryland

W. Virginia

Oklahoma

California

Neosho

New Orleans

U.S. Navy Pacific Headquarters

Helena

San Francisco

Oglala

Honolulu

submarines

Shaw

signal tower

Pennsylvania

dry docks

Downes

Cassin

U.S. Naval Station

OAHU

did Japan. In addition, Japanese fighting men, especially pilots, received more intensive training than did U.S. forces. With war on two fronts, the United States had to catch up quickly.

Immediately, the nation geared up for the fight. Young men enlisted in the military by the thousands. U.S. factories scrambled to produce ships, planes, tanks, and guns. In the months that followed, as more and more men left for war, factories and shipyards needed workers. So women stepped in to fill jobs usually held by men. They became experienced workers, including riveters, welders, and assemblers. Other civilians (people not in the military) volunteered for civil defense work—preparing their communities for air raids, watching for enemy planes, and patrolling the nation's shores for enemy ships. Across the nation, "Remember Pearl Harbor" became a rallying cry for the American people. They were united behind a single goal: to defeat the Axis powers.

The First Prisoner

After the bombing at Pearl Harbor, a dark-haired young man sat stone-faced in a chair. He refused to answer the questions the Americans were asking. He had three strange burn marks under each of his eyes, but his face was boyishly handsome. And he was short—about five feet three and a half inches tall, He probably reminded the Americans of a young teenager back home. But he was 24 years old and a graduate of the Japanese Naval Academy. He was also the first Japanese to be taken prisoner of war by the United States in World War II.

His name was Kazuo Sakamaki, and he had commanded a miniature two-man submarine (underwater vessel) sent to attack U.S. ships at Pearl Harbor. It was a suicide mission from which he was not expected to return, and he wished he had died. His only crewman, plus the eight men aboard four similar mini-submarines, had been killed in the attack. Japan would honor them as heroes. Their proud families would be honored too. But as a prisoner, Sakamaki had disgraced not only himself but also his entire family far away in Japan.

Sakamaki begged his U.S. captors to kill him. But they didn't. That would have violated the Geneva Convention, an 1864 treaty that established the international rules of war.

INTO THE THICK OF BATTLE

Following the attack on Pearl Harbor and other Pacific targets, the Japanese seemed to be moving forward in a well-planned strategy. But there was also disagreement among members of the Japanese High Command. Some Japanese admirals and generals wanted to take a break from the early assaults in order to protect areas they had already captured. But Admiral Yamamoto convinced them that Japan had to keep attacking before U.S. industry could begin to produce ships and planes at full speed. He wanted to move on to the Philippine Islands.

With more than 7,000 islands off the coast of Southeast Asia, the Philippine Islands cover 115,651 square miles and stretch 1,152 miles from north to south. The islands have many bays and harbors where ships can dock, but the United States considered the country most important as a base for aircraft.

Just north of the capital city of Manila, on the main island of Luzon, the United States had constructed Clark Field. There, the United States kept a fleet of B-17 bombers, known as Flying Fortresses. In addition, U.S. Army general Douglas MacArthur commanded a large force of U.S. and Filipino troops in the Philippines.

The Japanese High Command was nervous about a U.S. military base so close to its own country. So the day after the attack on Pearl Harbor, Japan had bombed Clark Field, destroying half the B-17s and 80 other U.S. planes on the ground. In one day, U.S. airpower near the Japanese homeland was almost totally eliminated. And with the U.S. planes destroyed, Japan was prepared and ready to launch a massive invasion of the Philippine Islands.

On December 10, Japan had landed a small number of troops on Luzon. Then 12 days later, Japan had sent its entire Fourteenth Army to attack the island. After two weeks of furious battle, the combined U.S. and Filipino forces were forced to retreat. More than 100,000 troops and civilians were driven back to the Bataan Peninsula west of Manila, where most didn't have enough food or water.

Unwilling to surrender, the Filipinos and their American defenders ate dogs and lizards, along with whatever roots and berries they could scavenge. They suffered from malnutrition and tropical ailments.

The sick and undernourished troops continued to fight for three months, even after President Roosevelt ordered General MacArthur to take command of U.S. forces elsewhere. Vowing, "I shall return," MacArthur reluctantly left for Australia on March 12, 1942, leaving General Jonathan Wainwright in charge of the troops in the Philippines. Starved and weak, 36,000 U.S. and Filipino troops at Bataan continued to resist until General Wainwright finally surrendered on April 9.

Some of the Allied troops escaped into the jungle. Others accompanied General Wainwright to the island of Corregidor, where he set up new defensive positions. But thousands of U.S. and Filipino soldiers were captured and became Japanese prisoners of war.

BRUTALITY AT BATAAN

American trucks were available to transport the Allied prisoners, but the Japanese chose to make them walk to a temporary prison camp. The route was 65 miles long, north from Mariveles on the Bataan Peninsula to the railroad at San Fernando, although distances for each prisoner varied according to where he was captured.

The march quickly became a massacre. The prisoners received no food or water as

Jungle Ailments

Servicemen in the Pacific suffered from a number of serious medical conditions. Some of these illnesses were common in tropical regions. Others were caused by malnutrition, or poor diets. These ailments included:

beriberi: a disease caused by a lack of thiamine (vitamin B1) in the diet. The illness is seen in people who are starving or whose diets lack enough whole grains, meat, nuts, potatoes, and green vegetables. Symptoms include numbness or a burning sensation in the legs. In severe cases, a patient may become paralyzed.

dysentery: a severe infection of the intestines that causes diarrhea, weakness, and abdominal pain. Acute dysentery can lead to dehydration and sometimes death.

jungle rot: a fungus that causes spreading sores on the skin. It is caused by intense humidity.

malaria: a serious disease spread by the bite of the anopheles mosquito. Malaria affects the kidneys, liver, brain, and blood. Symptoms include shaking, chills, and high fever. Malaria can be fatal.

scurvy: a condition caused by an inadequate amount of vitamin C in the diet. Symptoms include bleeding, bruising, and loosening of teeth. Fruits (especially citrus fruits) and vegetables are rich in vitamin C. Other sources of vitamin C are liver, kidneys, fish, and milk.

Bataan Death March
April 10–24, 1942

- - - - Route of the Death March
▬▬▬ Rail portion of the Death March
● City

Miles
0   10   20

0   10   20   30
Kilometers

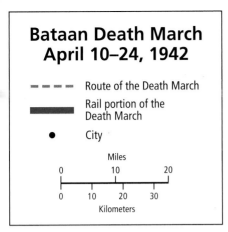

Philippine Islands

SOUTH CHINA SEA

LUZON

Philippine Sea

Area of map

Corregidor

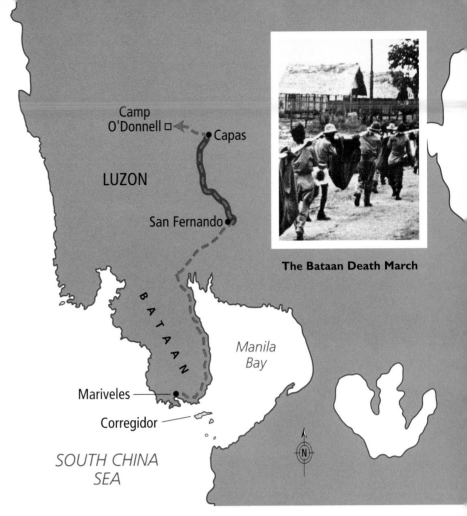

Camp O'Donnell □
Capas
LUZON
San Fernando ●
BATAAN
Manila Bay
Mariveles ─
Corregidor ─
SOUTH CHINA SEA
N

The Bataan Death March

they walked. Captors kicked men who fell from illness or exhaustion, occasionally breaking ribs or crushing internal organs. Some Japanese soldiers killed their victims with rifles and bayonets (blades attached to their rifles).

At San Fernando, the prisoners were put into train cars for a 20-mile ride to the town of Capas. They were packed in so tightly that no one could sit or lie down. Some died from their injuries or illnesses standing up, because there was no room to fall. Survivors of the ride were then marched 6 more miles to Camp O'Donnell.

Still the brutality continued. Prisoners who survived what came to be called the Bataan Death March were sent to slave labor camps throughout Japan, Korea, China, and the Philippines. According to Japanese beliefs of the time, only worthless cowards surrendered. Japanese captors, therefore, continued to treat the U.S. prisoners cruelly.

Altogether, 25,000 U.S. and Filipino troops died in the final hours of battle at Bataan and during the Death March that followed. For the rest of World War II, "Remember Bataan" became almost as familiar as "Remember Pearl Harbor."

THE DOOLITTLE RAID

Following the early Japanese victories, Allied commanders wanted to lift the sagging spirits of U.S. troops and civilians.

So Army Air Forces general Henry "Hap" Arnold, Admiral Ernest J. King (head of the U.S. Navy), and Admiral Chester W. Nimitz (commander of the Pacific Fleet) hatched a dangerous scheme. The plan was to send long-range B-25 bombers to Tokyo, the Japanese capital, and to the nearby cities of Yokohama and Nagoya. The planes would launch from an aircraft carrier named *Hornet*.

Hornet's deck wasn't long enough for the bombers to land there on a return flight, however. So after their strikes, the planes would continue on to air bases in China.

There, they would become the property of China, which was an official U.S. ally.

Lieutenant Colonel James H. Doolittle, a former World War I flight instructor, was chosen to organize and lead a crack team of Army Air Forces volunteers. He began at once to train 16 crews of five men each.

On April 2, 1942, USS *Hornet* set sail for a point in the Pacific 400 miles from Japan, where the planes would be launched two weeks later. Another carrier, USS *Enterprise*, the flagship (headquarters) of navy vice admiral William F. Halsey, joined *Hornet* on April 13. Fighter aircraft from *Enterprise*

USS *Hornet* steams toward a location about 400 miles off the coast of Japan in April 1942. *Hornet* carries B-25 bombers that will fly over Tokyo during the Doolittle Raid.

Crew members look on as a U.S. B-25 bomber roars from *Hornet*'s flight deck for its bombing run on Tokyo, Japan, during the 1942 Doolittle Raid.

were assigned to fly with *Hornet* to fight off any enemy planes that might approach.

Before dawn on the scheduled launch day, the Americans spotted enemy coast guard boats much farther east than expected. If the carrier moved in as close as originally planned, the planes were likely to be seen and counterattacked quickly. So the bombers would have to take off from *Hornet* while still more than 650 miles out to sea.

On April 18, the weather was perfect. In a strong wind that helped them lift from *Hornet*'s short flight deck, the bombers took off one at a time. Inside the cockpit of the first B-25, Doolittle himself led the way.

By a strange coincidence, Tokyo was holding its first air-raid drill (practice for an enemy air attack) when the U.S. bombers approached. Japanese citizens on the ground had never seen hostile aircraft

before. They assumed that the U.S. planes were a realistic touch that their own government had provided for the drill. Many people waved cheerfully at the low-flying planes—until the deadly cargoes of bombs shrieked down.

But the raid was not a big success. The bombs did not hit important targets, and damage to the buildings of Tokyo, Yokohama, and Nagoya was light. Of the 16 planes, 15 were shot down or forced to crash-land in China. Friendly Chinese tried to help the surviving crewmen sneak back across Japanese-held areas. But the Japanese captured eight men from two planes and executed three of them. One B-25 reached Vladivostok, Russia, part of the Soviet Union. The Soviets, not yet a U.S. ally, held the crew captive until they escaped more than a year later.

Although the raid wasn't a military victory, it caused anguish to members of the Japanese High Command. They were especially outraged that anyone would drop bombs near the palace of their god-like emperor in Tokyo. Meanwhile, across the Pacific, the U.S. military was jubilant over the success of catching the Japanese by surprise.

Believing that B-25s were too big and clumsy to launch from ships, the Japanese assumed that the United States had established secret air bases on Pacific islands. That worry ended the squabbling among members of the Japanese High Command. They agreed to Yamamoto's strategy of moving at once to crush the U.S. Navy, Japan's main obstacle to dominating the Pacific.

THE BATTLE OF THE CORAL SEA

The Japanese planned to invade Port Moresby on the island of New Guinea in May 1942. From there, they would be within easy bombing range of Australia, an important U.S. ally. But the United States had deciphered (broken) several codes that the Japanese commanders sent back and forth by radio. So the Americans knew in advance about the strike.

In previous wars, naval battles had involved huge battleships firing monstrous artillery (cannons and other big guns) at each other. But many U.S. battleships had

USS *Lexington* viewed from the deck of *Yorktown*. The ships are positioning to launch their aircraft against the Japanese fleet during the Battle of the Coral Sea in May 1942.

A Chinese soldier guards aircraft of the U.S. Flying Tigers squadron at an air base in China.

China-Burma-India

Although the major Asian battles of World War II took place on Pacific islands, some fighting occurred in the Asian nations of China, Burma (modern-day Myanmar), and India. Japan had first invaded China in 1931. With poorly trained troops and a shortage of weapons, China could do little to fight back. By 1942 Japan held much of eastern China. The Japanese also captured Chinese food supplies, creating widespread starvation in China. Political fighting within China further weakened the nation.

The other Allied nations tried to keep China in the fight. The United States sent pilots to China to attack Japanese forces from the air. These pilots included the famed Flying Tigers, led by army colonel Claire L. Chennault. The Allies also sent supplies and weapons to China by plane, flying "over the hump"—over the Himalayan Mountains—from India.

At first, the Allies also sent supplies overland. The shipments traveled from India to China through Burma, a former British colony. The route was called the Burma Road. But Japan conquered Burma in 1942 and closed the road. Led by British admiral Louis Mountbatten and U.S. general Joseph W. Stilwell, the Allies fought a series of bloody battles to win back Burma. Fighting through dense jungles, they finally reopened the Burma Road and regained Burma in 1945.

India served as an important supply and training center for the Allies during the war. Little fighting occurred on Indian soil, but the Japanese did invade several towns on India's eastern border in 1944. A British colony, India sent soldiers to fight in the Pacific as members of the Allies.

been sunk or severely damaged at Pearl Harbor. To defend Port Moresby, therefore, the United States planned to rely instead on planes launched from aircraft carriers.

In May 1942, three U.S. carriers were already in the western Pacific. Two of them—*Hornet* and *Lexington*—hurried to the Coral Sea, east of Australia, to join Australian ships as they waited for the Japanese fleet. To oppose those two U.S. aircraft carriers, the Japanese had three carriers. The two nations, however, had about the same number of planes and small warships.

At Work on the Home Front

With so many men off at war, Lorna Obermayr of Milwaukee, Wisconsin, knew that her father's machine shop was looking for help. Shortly after graduating from high school, she filled out an application and was hired as a welder. Standing only five feet two inches tall, she couldn't find steel-toed shoes small enough to fit her, so she wore a pair three sizes too big. "My small size was an advantage," she recalled many years later. "I could crawl inside those twenty foot long torpedo tubes to weld pretty easily."

As dawn broke on May 7, the skies were thick with ominous clouds. Both sides sent out aircraft to scout the locations of each other's ships. Then, with their slow and cumbersome Dauntless dive-bombers (planes that make steep dives toward a target before releasing their bombs), the Americans struck. The Japanese responded by launching their Zeros, fighter planes that could fly nearly 100 miles an hour faster than the awkward U.S. bombers. But the Dauntlesses were so ruggedly constructed that some continued diving even after being riddled with bullets.

This photograph taken from a USS *Lexington* plane shows the Japanese aircraft carrier *Shoho* on fire and sinking after direct bomb and torpedo hits during the Battle of the Coral Sea in 1942. *Lexington* would meet a similar fate only hours later.

The next morning, two bombs and two torpedoes (self-propelled explosive weapons that travel underwater) hit *Lexington*. Hundreds of men were killed and wounded as scorching fires blazed out of control. *Lexington*'s commander gave the order to abandon ship, and more than 2,000 men jumped into the water. Soon rescued by nearby vessels, many men wept uncontrollably as they watched their beloved "Lady Lex" slowly disappear into the sea.

The Japanese suffered similar losses. Of that nation's three carriers, *Shoho* was sunk, *Shokaku* was badly damaged, and *Zuikaku* lost most of its planes.

Neither side was able to claim a clear victory at the Coral Sea, but the battle prevented Japanese forces from invading Port Moresby. The battle also went down in the history books as the first naval combat during which enemy ships were never in sight of one another.

THE TIDE TURNS

2

Working in their windowless basement room in "the Dungeon" at Pearl Harbor in 1942, a U.S. Navy team had cracked several Japanese codes. That was how they knew in advance about the planned Japanese invasion of Port Moresby. Soon after that battle, the navy learned that another Japanese invasion was about to take place on an island the Japanese referred to as AF. But the Americans did not know what AF stood for.

Lieutenant Commander Joseph J. Rochefort was the leader of the navy's code-breaking team in the Pacific. He suspected that AF was the code name for the tiny island of Midway, where the Americans had an air base. He wasn't certain, however. So Rochefort's team came up with a clever plan to trick the Japanese into revealing the meaning of AF.

Located about 1,000 miles northwest of Pearl Harbor, Midway is an atoll, or coral island surrounding a lagoon. Because the island has no freshwater resources, water for cooking and drinking had to be brought in by ship or created by purifying seawater. Rochefort's code-breaking team suggested that the Americans send an uncoded message saying that the water purification plant on Midway Island had broken down. U.S. intelligence officers (in charge of gathering and evaluating information from the enemy) would then listen for the Japanese response.

Soon the U.S. intelligence team heard what it was waiting for. In talking about the Midway water shortage to one another, the Japanese commanders used the term *AF*. Rochefort and his team were joyful.

They knew they had cracked the code, and the assault would be on Midway.

THE JAPANESE PLAN

Unaware that the United States had cracked the code for Midway Island, Admiral Yamamoto was expecting another stunning victory like the one at Pearl Harbor. Before the attack on Midway, he gathered every available ship in the Japanese navy.

These ships included 11 battleships, the biggest and most powerful warships used in World War II. Their hulls (bodies) were protected by thick metal plates, and they carried huge guns and many torpedoes.

The Japanese also had 23 cruisers, the second most powerful ships used in the war. Fast and heavily armored, they were equipped with big guns and several torpedoes. The Japanese had 65 destroyers (ships armed with midsize guns and torpedoes) and 21 submarines, also armed with torpedoes. Finally, the Japanese had eight aircraft carriers. These carriers transported approximately 700 planes, including the agile Zero fighters.

To protect the U.S. air base on Midway, Admiral Nimitz was able to assemble only six heavy cruisers, one light cruiser, 17 destroyers, and three aircraft carriers with a total of 233 planes. Although the U.S. fleet had fewer vessels, it had one significant edge. Because the Americans knew that Yamamoto was planning to strike Midway, they had the advantage of surprise.

Yamamoto's final plan for Midway was complicated. He would send one task force (group of warships) north to the Aleutians, a chain of islands stretching hundreds of miles west into the Pacific from Alaska. He assumed that the U.S. fleet would follow the task force to the Aleutians, then be pounded by the Japanese. At the same time, another Japanese task force would hammer the base and harbor at Midway. After the battle in the Aleutians, the damaged U.S. fleet would limp to its closest harbor, at Midway. There, waiting Japanese ships and planes would completely destroy it.

Despite his brilliant mind, Yamamoto had not thought through all the possibilities. He wasn't aware that the Americans knew about the Japanese plan to assault Midway. Instead of sending the fleet to the Aleutians to follow the Japanese, Admiral Nimitz directed his ships to sail right to Midway.

Isoroku Yamamoto reviews battle plans. Admirals Nimitz and Yamamoto matched wits for control of the South Pacific.

SHOWDOWN AT MIDWAY

On June 4, the three U.S. aircraft carriers were stationed near Midway, where the Japanese didn't expect them. As the Americans waited, planes from four Japanese carriers roared skyward and began dropping bombs and torpedoes on Midway's harbor and airfield. The U.S. planes launched too, but they were no match for the Japanese aircraft. The spirited Japanese Zeros shot down two-thirds of the U.S. planes, while heavy Japanese bombers blasted U.S. hangars (garages for aircraft) and airstrips on the ground.

Things did not go as well for Japanese commanders on the four carriers, however. Because of sketchy reports from their pilots, they weren't sure if any U.S. carriers were nearby. The commanders began giving conflicting orders. First, they told deck crews to load their planes with torpedoes to assault U.S. ships. Then they backtracked

Midway Island

Midway got its name when the United States annexed (took control of) the island in 1867. It was called Midway because it is located in the middle of the Pacific Ocean. This location made Midway strategically important in World War II. It was a good stopping-off and refueling point for airplanes flying across the ocean, so the United States built an air base there. The Japanese wanted the island so they could use the air base to launch strikes at Hawaii and other Allied territory in the Pacific.

Canopies (cockpit covers) open for clear visibility, U.S. Dauntless dive-bombers from *Hornet* bank into their approach to the Japanese cruiser *Mikuma* (streaming a long plume of smoke at bottom center) during the Battle of Midway on June 6, 1942. This third strike on the cruiser sent it to the bottom.

and told the crews to load the planes with bombs to attack the air base once again. As a result of the confusion, Japanese carrier decks were covered with live bombs and torpedoes, waiting to be loaded into planes.

Flying beneath thick clouds, the first wave of U.S. warplanes spotted the Japanese ships. The aircraft flew low to launch their torpedoes, but before they could complete their attack, antiaircraft fire and swooping Japanese fighter planes destroyed most of them.

At nearly the same time, a second wave of U.S. bombers dived out of high cloud cover directly over the battle. With the attention of the Japanese on the first wave, they took the Japanese by surprise. The U.S. airmen bombed and destroyed three Japanese carriers in only a few minutes. Live bombs and torpedoes stored on the flaming carrier decks exploded like giant firecrackers.

Once the position of the Japanese fleet became known, U.S. commanders desperately attacked with every airplane available from their carriers and from the "unsinkable carrier" of Midway Island. The Japanese struck back with their remaining air squadrons.

During the rest of the day, swarms of Japanese and U.S. pilots riddled each other's airplanes with bullets and slammed explosive payloads into enemy ships. Planes tumbled into the sea. Smoke-filled skies were reddened by blazing oil fires. Huge ships—both Japanese and American—listed

---

EYEWITNESS QUOTE: FROM MIDWAY ISLAND

"We opened on them [shot at the Japanese bombers] and pretty soon one of them came out of the formation burning. It fell into the sea. Several others fell out also. In all, I actually saw four fall."

—M. Wayne Silker, pharmacist's mate (naval medic), U.S. Navy

(tilted to one side) at crazy angles and sank.

A TURNING POINT

Men on both sides were bloody and exhausted when a torpedo struck USS *Yorktown*. The ship sank. But that was the only carrier the Americans lost. Other losses included a destroyer, about 150 planes, and 307 men.

The U.S. casualties were devastating, but Yamamoto's were far more serious. The carriers *Kaga* and *Akagi* had sunk immediately after the battle began. *Soryu* had soon followed. Only *Hiryu* had remained upright long enough for a final, devastating launch of aircraft against the U.S forces. Altogether, the Japanese lost four carriers, a heavy cruiser, three destroyers, 322 planes, and more than 5,000 men. The human loss was the most significant because Japan was never able to replace its rigorously trained pilots. It didn't have enough airplane fuel to continue the intensive training that Japanese airmen had received in the past.

At Midway the United States had won its first decisive battle in the Pacific. The war would continue, but the tide of battle had turned. U.S. factories were quickly churning out ships and planes to replace wartime losses. Yamamoto had been right to fear America's industrial strength.

SIX MONTHS IN THE SOLOMONS

Thousands of U.S. Marines stepped over the railings of 50 troopships that had brought them to the Solomon Islands,

Seabees

The navy's Construction Battalion was established in December 1941. Its members, called Seabees (for "CB"—the Construction Battalion's initials), had skill in construction, and their mission was to build as well as to fight. Using bulldozers and other mechanical equipment, they built airstrips, hospitals, docks, roads, and bridges almost overnight. Sometimes, the Seabees defended these same facilities from enemy attack. The navy also assigned the Seabees to hazard duty, handling explosives and scouting minefields.

located east of New Guinea in the Pacific Ocean. Bobbing on the ocean below them were hundreds of landing craft, small

armored boats that would transport the men closer to shore.

Cautiously, the marines climbed down nets of heavy rope, which shifted dangerously under the weight and movement of so many climbers. The descent was steep and several stories high, so the men tried not to look down. They had to get safely into the small boats before the enemy started shooting. Then they could get their own rifles into position to return fire.

The date was August 7, 1942, and the marines were part of U.S. Task Force 61. They were about to participate in the first U.S. land attack in the Pacific. Under the command of Major General Alexander Vandegrift, the men were expected to retake the Solomons, a British-controlled territory that Japan had seized in December 1941.

Japanese torpedo bombers approach low and through U.S. antiaircraft fire to attack landing craft of Task Force 61 during the U.S. invasion of the Solomons in August 1942. U.S. servicemen called these aircraft "Betty" bombers.

It was a big and challenging assignment. Most of the marines had never been in combat before or even seen a tropical jungle outside a Hollywood movie.

The 50 U.S. troopships, with 19,000 marines aboard, anchored at Savo Sound, toward the southwest of the Solomon chain. Landing-craft pilots then steered their boatloads of marines in two directions: some to a group of four small islands including Tulagi and others to the much larger island of Guadalcanal. Then the pilots ran into unsuspected coral reefs, which blocked their progress toward the islands. So struggling under the 40-pound loads that they carried on their backs, the troops clambered out of the boats and into the water.

Holding their rifles out of the water, they sloshed toward the dense jungles ahead. By the time they reached the beaches, their green uniforms and canvas leggings were soppy as dishrags. Their toes squished inside their heavy, water-soaked combat boots.

After wading to the sand that first day, the marines rested under towering coconut palm trees before pushing farther on. In addition to the suffocating heat, everything about the jungle seemed unfriendly. Dank air filled the men's nostrils. Sharp grasses tore at bare skin. Snakes and leeches slithered underfoot. But worst of all were the insects. Swarms of them were everywhere. They buzzed and thrummed. They tickled and bit. They even sucked their way into ears and noses. Especially dangerous were the anopheles mosquitoes, whose bites could cause the potentially fatal disease malaria.

U.S. Marines wade ashore at Tulagi in August 1942. Fierce fighting for the island followed.

THE TULAGI INVASION

At Tulagi the U.S. Marines awed the Japanese defenders with their numbers and ferocity. Members of Colonel Merritt A. Edson's First Raider Battalion pushed forward, destroying Japanese artillery and men. But the Japanese were equally determined. Vowing to fight to the last man, they charged the Americans with bayonets. Rushing forward, they yelled, "Banzai! Banzai!" That shout, meaning "ten thousand years," was an ecstatic cheer made in hopes that the Japanese emperor would live that long. The Americans answered with hand grenades and shellfire, until the Japanese ran for cover in caves and crevices for the night.

Reinvigorated the next morning, the Japanese fought desperately to stop the advancing Americans. From inside their caves, they sent a barrage of gunfire and hand grenades. But the Americans had greater numbers and better weapons. With cannons shelling Japanese caves, they sent the enemy fleeing. Although the fighting was fierce, marines were able to force Japanese fighters off Tulagi Island in just three days.

INVASION AT GUADALCANAL

Things did not go as well on Guadalcanal. It is a kidney-shaped island, approximately 90 miles wide by 125 miles long. Earlier that summer, the pilot of a U.S. scout plane had spotted Japanese troops building an air base on the island, near a strip of land called Lunga Point. U.S. commanders realized that a base for enemy aircraft on the Solomons posed a serious threat to the United States and its allies. Australia, the United States' major ally in the South Pacific, was located dangerously close. Any ships carrying supplies and men to or from Australia would risk attack from Japanese planes. It was crucial for the marines to invade Guadalcanal and capture the airfield from the Japanese.

Landing on Guadalcanal, the men of the First and Third Battalions, Fifth Marines, met very little opposition. After wading to Red Beach on Lunga Point, the officers and

U.S. forces land at Guadalcanal in the Solomon Islands in 1942. Their objective: seize the island and take control of a Japanese-held airfield near Lunga Point.

men pushed farther south. When the marines reached the unfinished airfield, they saw that the workers there had fled. But in their haste, the enemy had abandoned huge stores of ammunition, gasoline, and radio equipment, plus tons of rice that was crawling with worms. Unaware that the construction workers were mostly forced laborers from Korea, not Japanese soldiers, the Americans were pleased with what seemed to be an easy victory.

At sites near the airfield, U.S. officers ordered the marines to dig foxholes— protective holes in the ground. When night fell, the marines were exhausted from their march and labors. Grateful for the protection of their foxholes, they climbed inside to sleep.

Suddenly, they heard ear-splitting bursts of gunfire. Green lights flashed. Startled awake, the marines realized that U.S. and Australian ships off Savo Island, a tiny outcropping of land near Guadalcanal, were under attack. Under cover of darkness, a Japanese force of five heavy cruisers, two light cruisers, and a destroyer had slipped through the Slot, a narrow passage between two minor chains of the Solomons.

Among the ships under attack were the transports that had brought the marines to the Solomons. Caught unprepared, those ships were now understaffed. Rear Admiral Richmond K. Turner, who commanded

> **EYEWITNESS QUOTE: ON GUADALCANAL**
>
> "When the Condition Red [alarm] sirens sounded we extinguished lights. Then we put on our helmets and lay on our bellies in those dank foxholes. . . . When you are on your belly in a foxhole there is nothing which will hold your undivided attention like an aerial bomb whistling and screaming its way toward you."
>
> —Lawrence Cracroft, captain, U.S. Marine Corps

them, notified General Vandegrift that he would have to leave the area. But because he had not finished unloading supplies for the marines who had already landed on Guadalcanal, the men on the island were stranded. They had enough food for only 37 days and enough ammunition for just four days of heavy fighting.

The furious naval attack lasted only 40 minutes, but it was a serious defeat for the U.S. forces. When the victorious Japanese withdrew from the Slot, they had suffered only light casualties and minor damage to three ships. Thirty-seven Japanese sailors had been killed, and another 57 had been wounded.

Caught in enemy searchlights, USS *Quincy* cannot hide from Japanese attacks during the Battle of Savo Island in 1942. *Quincy* sank during the fight.

But the losses to the U.S. and Australian forces were staggering. Human destruction amounted to 1,250 sailors killed and 750 wounded. Four cruisers had been sunk, and a cruiser and a destroyer had been badly damaged. In fact, so many ships had been sunk that the area became known as Ironbottom Sound.

REBUILDING HENDERSON FIELD

Following such a one-sided battle, morale plummeted among U.S. troops on Guadalcanal. Because food supplies were short, meals were limited to only two a day. The men had no choice but to eat the wormy rice that the Korean laborers at the airfield had abandoned.

Nevertheless, the marines set to work rebuilding the airfield. The troops realized that once it was finished and in U.S. hands, U.S. aircraft could use it to deliver desperately needed provisions. The planes could also provide air support in battles that might occur in New Guinea or on the Solomon, Gilbert, or Marshall Islands.

The men strung a barbed-wire fence around the field, in a huge arc that curved from the beach into the jungle, then back again to the beach. They set up machine guns along the fence. Although the fence offered protection against Japanese attacks by land, it could not protect the men from enemy ships and planes. Without fighter planes or antiaircraft ammunition, the

Marines captured Henderson Field *(above)* after sustaining heavy losses during the bloody fighting on Guadalcanal in 1942. Their capture of the airfield moved U.S. aircraft closer to Japanese targets. Fighting continued, however, as Japanese forces attempted to retake the important airfield.

American troops were vulnerable. Japanese bombs fell not only on the unfinished airfield but also near foxholes.

Although it might have seemed like an eternity to the hungry troops, six days after the Battle of Savo Island, the marines at the airfield finally received provisions. During the night of August 14, Admiral Turner sent four ships up the Slot with food, gasoline, and ammunition. Also aboard were 123 Seabees. With their expert help, the marines at Lunga Point were able to complete the airfield on August 18. They named it Henderson Field in honor of Lofton Henderson, a marine pilot who had died at Midway.

The military code name for the humid island of Guadalcanal was Cactus, and bombers and fighter planes taking off and landing at Henderson Field became known as the Cactus Air Force. After the airfield was completed, land assaults, some very bloody, continued on the island. But the marines and other ground forces felt secure in knowing that the "Cactus boys" would provide air cover. The planes were able to drive back some of the Japanese troopships that approached the island.

THE BATTLE OF BLOODY RIDGE

One of the fiercest battles in the next few months occurred between September 12 and 14 at a ridge south of Henderson Field. Six thousand Japanese troops from General Harukichi Hyakutake's Seventeenth Army arrived at the island in a series of ships known as the Tokyo Express.

Determined to regain the airfield they had once started building, the Japanese

Japanese soldiers lie dead following the Battle of Bloody Ridge in September 1942. Both sides saw heavy losses in the fight to secure Henderson Field, but the Japanese sustained the worst casualties.

faced bitter combat with the Lunga Point troops. The U.S. force included marines from Colonel Merritt Edson's First Raider Battalion. Edson and his men had recently come to Guadalcanal from Tulagi Island and were positioned at a ridge south of Henderson Field.

The Americans ousted the occupying Japanese, although 260 Americans were killed or wounded. The Japanese lost about four times that number. So many troops lost their lives in just three days that the area came to be known as Bloody Ridge.

LIFE ON THE HOME FRONT

When the United States went to war in December 1941, life changed for all Americans. The war brought an end to the Great Depression, a period when one out of four U.S. workers couldn't find a job. Suddenly, after Pearl Harbor, the country geared up to mass-produce weapons such as rifles, warships and tanks. Factory and other jobs were plentiful.

Americans had more money to spend than they had had during the Depression years, but there was little to buy. All extra food, fabric, and metal were needed to feed, clothe, and make weapons for the troops fighting overseas. Women had difficulty finding stockings because nylon and silk were needed to make parachutes. Cotton was needed for uniforms and bandages. A woman from Pocatello, Idaho, remembered the empty shelves in grocery stores during the war: "When we heard by word of mouth that [the grocery store] had bananas, all of us housewives flocked down to grab a few."

BUY WAR BONDS

A government poster urges U.S. citizens to buy bonds to help pay for the war.

To make do, mothers cut and resewed old adult clothes to make them fit children. The government encouraged people to grow their own vegetables. Homeowners dug up their flower beds to plant "Victory Gardens," filled with carrots, beets, beans, and tomatoes. In 1943 homegrown produce accounted for one-third of all the vegetables eaten that year.

Meat, sugar, coffee, and dairy products were rationed (sold in limited amounts). People received books of ration stamps to turn in with money at the grocery store. The system allowed each member of a household to buy only about two pounds of meat or fish per week. Shoes were limited to two pairs per person per year.

Gasoline was also rationed, so people drove less. Motorists received a windshield sticker with a letter ranging from *A* to *E*. Anyone could get an A sticker, which allowed the driver three gallons of gas a week. But only people whose cars were necessary for their work—such as police officers and doctors—were entitled to an E sticker. Rubber was even scarcer than gas, and tires were needed for military vehicles. Once a motorist's tires wore out, it was almost impossible to purchase more. No one could buy a new car because automobile factories made army trucks and tanks instead of cars for civilians.

Everyone pitched in. Schoolchildren went through their neighborhoods collecting old pans and other scrap metal that could be melted down and made into guns and ammunition. The U.S. government urged all citizens to purchase war bonds, which was like making a loan to the government. For instance, a

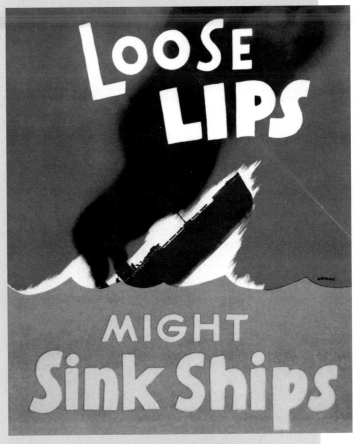

Posters like this one warned U.S. citizens to keep silent about military information.

bond costing $18.75 could be sold back to the government 10 years later for $25. Bonds were available in values up to $10,000. Anyone who didn't have enough money to purchase a bond could save up to buy one by placing stamps worth 10 or 25 cents in a savings book. Schools and social groups often competed to see who could sell the most bonds or stamps.

Civilians sometimes complained about the inconveniences of World War II. But most were willing to make sacrifices to help the war effort. To encourage citizens to pitch in, the government produced propaganda posters, with messages promoting the American cause. One poster told civilians that "Loose Lips Might Sink Ships"—which meant that no one should talk about military matters, since spies could be listening. A more common poster showed a whiskered man (Uncle Sam) pointing a finger and saying, "I Want You for the U.S. Army."

THE FINAL BATTLE

Approximately 12,000 Japanese troops remained on Guadalcanal, hedged in and outnumbered by U.S. forces. On November 13, the Japanese made a determined attempt to rescue these men. That night, two Japanese battleships came down the Slot, planning to land troops on the island. But they encountered U.S. ships.

The bay erupted in booming, fiery explosions. Shells arched from ship to ship. Gunfire whistled and roared. Ships listed and sank.

Outnumbered, U.S. forces fought desperately, sinking one of the two enemy battleships. But the United States lost two cruisers, one of which was *Juneau,* with five brothers aboard. They were members of the Sullivan family from Iowa. They survived the sinking only to die awaiting rescue.

The following night, Japan tried again to land its troops. This time, the Japanese

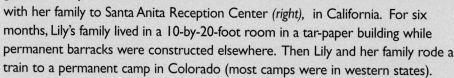

Japanese American Internment

In February 1942, fearing that Japanese Americans might spy for Japan, the U.S. government authorized the internment (imprisonment) of Japanese Americans living in western states. By 1943 about 123,000 Japanese Americans were interned in camps.

Yuriko (Lily) Nakai, a Japanese American girl, was nine years old when she was bused with her family to Santa Anita Reception Center *(right),* in California. For six months, Lily's family lived in a 10-by-20-foot room in a tar-paper building while permanent barracks were constructed elsewhere. Then Lily and her family rode a train to a permanent camp in Colorado (most camps were in western states).

As children, with fewer memories of freedom, Lily and her brother George adjusted better than most adults to life at their camp. They attended classes in the barracks schoolroom. George joined the Boy Scouts, and Lily played piano the school orchestra.

Their mother, who had managed to bring her sewing machine to camp, taught sewing classes to some of the other women and girls. She earned $16 a month to buy needed items—heavy jackets, boots, eyeglasses—plus extras such as books and yarn from the Montgomery Ward catalog. She also gained self-esteem.

However, Lily's father grew restless and angry. He had nothing to do. His skills as a gardener were useless at the dusty camp. He resented the strict rules and the endless lines for meals and showers. He scowled at the barbed wire keeping him a prisoner. In time he received permission to leave the camp and look for work elsewhere, only occasionally returning to visit his family. In August 1945, the U.S. government began closing the camps. The process took six months.

The Sullivan Brothers

The U.S. military tried to avoid assigning siblings to the same unit. However, five brothers from Waterloo, Iowa, were allowed to serve together. The Sullivans *(right)*— George, 28; Francis, 27; Joseph, 24; Madison, 23; and Albert, 20—were all aboard USS *Juneau* when it sank in the naval battle of Guadalcanal on November 13, 1942. Among 140 crew members who managed to get into rubber life rafts, the brothers drifted at sea until they died of hunger, thirst, and exposure.

Their sister, Genevieve, later became a WAVE (a member of the navy's women's reserve unit). But like all women in the military at the time, she did not hold a combat position.

the five Sullivan brothers "missing in action" off the Solomons

THEY DID THEIR PART

force was met by a U.S. fleet commanded by Admiral Willis A. Lee. By dawn of November 15, the Americans had forced the enemy ships to retreat. With no help available, the remaining Japanese troops stayed on Guadalcanal for nearly three more months.

During the first week of February 1943, a series of Japanese destroyers landed in the blackness of night at Cape Esperance on the island's northwestern tip. With those ships, Japan evacuated the 12,000 troops. By February 9, six months after the U.S. invasion, all Japanese fighting men had departed. At Guadalcanal, the United States had scored its first successful land offensive in the Pacific.

ISLAND HOPPING

3

In the two years after the attack on Pearl Harbor, the U.S. Pacific Fleet had grown strong. With hundreds of versatile planes and scores of aircraft carriers to transport them, Admiral Nimitz was ready to begin Operation Galvanic in November 1943. That was the code name for the U.S. strategy of island hopping (seizing key islands, from which attacks on other islands could be launched) westward to Japan. Nimitz appointed capable officers to help in the planning. They included Vice Admiral Raymond A. Spruance, Rear Admiral Richmond K. Turner, and Major General Holland M. "Howlin' Mad" Smith.

Soon thousands of troops were headed toward a group of small islands called Tarawa, part of the Gilbert Islands chain. Tarawa's main island, Betio, held a Japanese airfield, which the Americans wanted. From it, they could launch planes still farther west.

Betio, just three miles long by 500 yards wide, was defended by 5,000 Japanese troops. Crouched inside pillboxes (artillery stations) constructed of coconut logs, sand, concrete, and steel, the defenders waited. Meanwhile, U.S. amtracs (vehicles that could travel on both land and water) got caught in the reef around the island and had to drop off their loads of marines early. Carrying heavy gear and pressing through chest-deep water, the Americans were easy targets for Japanese snipers (gunmen hiding from view). Some of the invading marines got caught in barbed wire, and all faced machine-gun fire as they struggled forward. As some of their comrades disappeared under water that churned blood red, thousands of attackers kept coming.

Once onshore, the Americans could return the fire that had been coming toward them. The fighting escalated. After three days of grim battle and 3,000 casualties, the marines captured Betio. The enemy losses were greater. Only 17 of 5,000 Japanese defenders survived the close-quarter combat. (Following Japanese codes of honor, many committed suicide rather than surrender.)

In February 1944, the Americans moved on to the Marshall Islands. In the process of securing the island of Kwajalein, the Americans suffered nearly 2,000 casualties out of 41,000 troops. But they killed almost all of the 8,400 Japanese defenders on the island. Two weeks later, at Enewetak Atoll, the United States counted up 1,200 more casualties and killed nearly all of the 3,500 Japanese defenders.

BATTLES OF THE MARIANAS

Still ahead for the Americans were the Mariana Islands, including Saipan, Tinian, and Guam. Capturing these islands would bring U.S. forces even closer to Japan. Saipan, the first target, was a thriving tropical island. It had many sugar plantations run mainly by immigrant Japanese farmers, who sold their sugar to Japan. The Japanese outnumbered the native islanders, called Chamorros, by about nine to one.

Protecting the plantations and civilians on Saipan was an army of 25,000 men under General Yoshitsugo Saito, who commanded all the Japanese troops on the Marianas. Also available were 6,000 naval

troops under Vice Admiral Chuichi Nagumo. The Japanese High Command expected the Americans to make a beach invasion on Saipan, as they had done at Guadalcanal and Tulagi.

Before invading an island, U.S. forces "softened up" enemy beaches by bombing and shelling them from planes and ships. This tactic destroyed enemy defenses and made it safer for U.S. troops to wade ashore. On June 13, 1944, Americans softened up Saipan with naval bombardments near Tanapag Harbor. The Japanese naturally expected the major U.S. invasion to take place there. However, the Tanapag strikes were designed to fool the Japanese.

U.S. bombers prepare to take off from USS Monterey to "soften up" Tinian Island in 1944.

SOLDIERS AND UNIFORMS

With war raging in Europe, the U.S. Congress established the country's first peacetime draft (a system for calling up young men into the military) in 1940. All American males ages to 21 to 35 (later, ages 18 to 44) were required to register for military service. In the beginning, drafted men had to serve one year in the army. With the attack on Pearl Harbor, the length of service was extended to the war's end, plus six months.

After the attack, many young Americans were eager to fight for their country. The draft called young men into the army. But men could also volunteer for the U.S. Army, U.S. Navy, or U.S. Marine Corps before their draft notices arrived, as many did. Some women also volunteered for military service, but they served in special women's reserve units. They were not allowed to hold combat jobs. In total, 16 million American men and women served in the military during World War II. All of the women enlisted, while two-thirds of the men were draftees.

Processing (testing and paperwork) took place at various military bases around the United States. After taking a physical exam, each soldier received a uniform, including underwear, black leather shoes, socks, a cap, and a helmet. Men heading toward the humid Pacific islands received a Class C uniform, or "chino"—a long-sleeved khaki (tan) shirt and tan trousers. In combat, troops

These U.S. Marine Raiders are wearing full tropical combat gear. Because of the extreme jungle heat, many soldiers (from both sides) shed as much gear as possible, often fighting shirtless.

wore heavy boots and lightweight olive green uniforms, colored with green and brown splotches, which made the men less visible in the jungle. Besides his uniform, each soldier typically received an M1 Garand rifle, a semiautomatic weapon capable of firing eight cartridges before it had to be reloaded.

Each soldier took basic training, during which he learned first of all to obey orders. Training also included tough exercises to improve physical fitness and lessons in battlefield tactics and handling explosives and weapons. Following basic

This U.S. government poster identifies Japanese uniforms and insignia (symbols showing rank).

training, each soldier learned to do a job such as repairing airplanes, driving tanks, or making maps. Some men were then sent overseas, while others worked behind the scenes at military bases in the United States.

JAPAN'S MILITARY

Japan also had a military draft, but it was less necessary than the draft in the United States. Most Japanese men were eager to join the military. They dreamed of bringing honor to themselves and their families by performing valiantly in battle. They believed that dying for the emperor would assure them a place in heaven and make their families proud.

Training for Japanese soldiers (especially pilots) lasted longer and was far more difficult than training for U.S. servicemen. At the beginning of the war, when Japan still had enough fuel, pilot trainees spent much more time in the air than did their U.S. counterparts.

Japanese soldiers wore khaki shirts and trousers, canvas shoes, and puttees, or strips of cloth wrapped around their ankles. Beneath their steel helmets, they wore khaki field caps with neck flaps that tied under the chin. Badges pinned to red collar patches showed each man's rank. Each Japanese infantryman carried a single-shot bolt-action rifle. Because this rifle required frequent reloading, it was much less effective than the M1 and M14 rifles typically given to U.S. troops.

U.S. Marines fight their way inland, toward Mount Tapotchau on Saipan. Fallen Japanese soldiers lie around the men. The fight to control Saipan is considered one of the deadliest battles of World War II.

The real invasion occurred two days later and farther south, at the beaches of Afetna Point and Charon Kanoa. There, waves of marines under Lieutenant General Holland M. Smith came ashore. They ruthlessly pushed their way toward Mount Tapotchau, a 1,550-foot peak in the center of Saipan. More marines arrived with the Army's Twenty-seventh Infantry Division, under General Ralph Smith, to capture Aslito airfield.

For three weeks, the fighting on Saipan was among the most ferocious in the Pacific. Eventually, army and marine troops firmly established themselves on Mount Tapotchau. Yet the bloodshed continued. Unwilling to surrender, desperate Japanese troops staged hopeless attacks. Crazed with too much of an alcoholic drink called sake, they rushed toward U.S. troops, yelling, "Banzai! Banzai!" Many had no guns and used whatever weapons they could find— hand grenades, bayonets on long sticks, or simple wooden clubs. But the Americans were better equipped, and Japanese casualties were very high.

THE AFTERMATH OF BATTLE

Humiliated by defeat, General Saito prepared for hara-kiri, an honorable, ritual method of suicide used for centuries by Japanese warriors. On July 7, kneeling on the floor of his command post, he took out his sword. After shouting, "Hurrah for the emperor!" he plunged the weapon into his abdomen. Another officer then shot him in the head before killing himself. Elsewhere on the island, Vice Admiral Nagumo, the naval commander, committed suicide too.

One month later, on July 10, U.S. troops officially raised the U.S. flag over Saipan. But the horror was far from over. U.S. forces tried to persuade surviving Japanese troops, as well as Japanese and Chamorro civilians, to surrender. Over loudspeakers, the Americans promised to treat prisoners well. But they also sometimes used flamethrowers that incinerated (burned up) soldiers and civilians inside the caves.

Some Japanese soldiers hid in caves and continued battling as snipers. Many more followed Saito's example and killed themselves with guns, knives, or hand grenades held against their stomachs. Many civilians also chose suicide. Some Japanese parents tossed their children off the 800-foot cliffs at

Hara-kiri

Samurai, traditional Japanese warriors, once practiced a ritual kind of suicide, known as hara-kiri, when they were disgraced. The warrior first obtained permission from the emperor to kill himself in this sacred manner. Then, while kneeling on the ground, the warrior stuck his sword into his abdomen and disemboweled himself (carved out his internal organs). By World War II, Japanese officers were no longer following this practice. Yet some officers, such as General Saito when he killed himself at Saipan, performed modified versions of the ritual.

Marpi Point before leaping themselves. Sometimes whole families waded or swam into the ocean to drown.

A marine on patrol discovers a family hiding in a cave on Saipan. Horrified by the gruesome fighting and fearing for their lives, civilians sought refuge in caves and tunnels on Saipan and other Pacific islands.

HARDWARE AND ARMAMENTS

Ships By December 1941, Japan had built the most powerful navy in the world. Some Japanese battleships were armed with bigger guns than any U.S. ships. Two Japanese superbattleships carried 18-inch guns. They were powerful enough to tear a crewman's clothes off his body if he were standing nearby when they were fired. The Japanese fleet also included aircraft carriers, cruisers, destroyers, and submarines.

Many U.S. battleships were destroyed at Pearl Harbor. Therefore, the Americans did not rely on battleships during the Pacific war. U.S. destroyers, equipped with ten torpedoes and as many as 10 five-inch guns, were fast and fairly powerful. Smaller destroyer escorts carried just three torpedoes and two five-inch guns. Although slower, they turned in a tighter circle than destroyers, which made them more efficient in attacking enemy submarines. They could also pick up

U.S. Carrier Task Group 38.3

airmen who fell into the water and could shoot antiaircraft fire. Large U.S. aircraft carriers usually held 50 to 100 planes. The main U.S. aircraft carriers were *Lexington, Saratoga, Hornet, Wasp, Enterprise,* and *Yorktown.* By 1943 U.S. shipbuilders were converting smaller merchant (trading) ships into vessels for carrying planes. Known officially as escort carriers, they were also called baby flattops or Jeep carriers. Designed for many uses, including escorting convoys and assisting troop landings, they were too small to launch or recover planes with ease, but they did carry about 25 planes and nine to twelve torpedoes.

Aircraft Japanese planes dominated the skies until late 1942. The Zero was an outstanding Japanese fighter. It could fly at 330 miles per hour and was far more agile than early U.S. planes. But it had two major weaknesses. It wasn't heavily armored, and it could go up in flames if a bullet punctured its fuel tank. The Japanese arsenal of aircraft also included bombers and dive-bombers. Early U.S. planes were more heavily armored and had self-sealing fuel tanks. But they were less maneuverable than Japan's planes. The Devastator was a torpedo bomber that

Mitsubishi A6M Zero

launched from a carrier. It was heavy and because of its outdated engine, it was slower than Japanese bombers. It was ineffective at Midway and was soon discarded. The Wildcat fighter was clumsy when compared to the Japanese Zero and also had a much shorter flight range. It, too, was discarded. Slowly replaced, the Dauntless dive-bomber was an early U.S. model that lasted throughout the war. Sturdy and strong, it could withstand heavy fire. It had a maximum speed of 250 miles per hour. Thought to be inappropriate for carrier operations, the U.S. Navy assigned the Corsair F4U attack aircraft to the Marine Corps for land-based flights. Armed with six machine guns, bombs and, later, rockets, the Corsair proved itself a formidable plane. In addition to its armaments, the plane was fast and could fly long distances. The Marine Corps relied heavily on the Corsair to soften enemy positions and to provide air support during its island

Corsair F4U

hopping campaign in the South Pacific. The B-25 was a medium bomber used for the Doolittle Raid on Japan in April 1942. The Avenger became the main U.S. torpedo plane during the war. In the Pacific, it was used primarily against Japanese merchant vessels. By late summer 1943, the Hellcat fighter had replaced the Wildcat. Able to outperform the Zero, it contributed greatly to American success in the war. The B-29 Superfortress, a four-engine bomber, was the most advanced bomber of World War II. It was used in 1945 to drop atomic bombs on the Japanese cities of Hiroshima and Nagasaki.

Advanced Technology Superior detection equipment contributed significantly to American success in the war. Sonar (whose name was created from the term *sound navigation and ranging*) was a system for detecting objects in water. A transmitter sent out sound waves in a 360-degree circle. If the waves hit something in the water, such as a submarine or a submerged portion of an iceberg, an echoing wave returned, telling operators the object's location.

Radar (from the term *radio detection and ranging*) was a similar system for detecting objects above water, such as ships and airplanes. Radar systems sent out radio waves instead of sound waves. Upgraded throughout the war, most U.S. combat planes and ships carried radar systems by 1943. But Japan did not have much radar equipment, and what it did have was inferior. Japan instead chose to develop and rely on night vision technology, which was superior to similar U.S. technology.

One Soldier's Story

H. Michael Moss, the son of a U.S. businessman, had been born in Tokyo. Until age 17, he lived in Japan, so he spoke both English and Japanese fluently. Moss became a U.S. Army captain. He was assigned to a Marine Corps division at Saipan and worked there with the team of Americans persuading the Japanese to surrender.

Learning about a cave full of Japanese near the hill where he was camped, Moss called to the people inside the cave. He realized that they were Chamorro civilians, not Japanese soldiers. The Japanese had told the Chamorros that the Americans would hurt them if they surrendered. So the Chamorros were too frightened to come out of the cave.

After considerable reassurance from Moss, the leader of the Chamorros finally emerged from the cave. He was bleeding profusely from two cuts in his neck. He had made the cuts himself, attempting to commit suicide, but the cuts were superficial. In time, Moss persuaded the other Chamorros inside the cave to come out too. All were suffering from intense stomach pain because they had swallowed laundry tablets, also trying to kill themselves. Many were too weak to walk to the medical facilities about a half mile away, so Moss and a marine companion carried them to the U.S. fort.

A team of U.S. soldiers convinces Japanese civilians to leave a Saipan cave.

While the many suicides were taking place, a small team of U.S. soldiers who could speak Japanese arrived at Saipan. These soldiers could talk personally with the Japanese and were therefore more persuasive than the blaring loudspeakers. They entered the caves where soldiers and civilians were holed up and convinced many of them not to take their own lives. One member of that team, a Japanese American named Ben Honda, received a Silver Star for his courage in entering enemy caves. Once inside, he was able to assure the Japanese that they would be treated well if they surrendered.

Human casualties on Saipan were enormous. Although no estimate could be made of the Japanese who had killed themselves by drowning, 23,811 Japanese bodies were counted and buried on land. Another 1,780 Japanese were taken as prisoners of war. The United States counted

3,426 of its own troops dead and 13,099 wounded.

Details of the Saipan defeat soon reached the Japanese High Command in Tokyo. On July 18, Prime Minister Hideki Tojo resigned with his entire cabinet (group of top advisers). Succeeding Tojo as prime minister was Kuniaki Koiso, who wondered if it was wise to continue the war. But he didn't express his doubts openly because the possibility of surrender was unthinkable to most Japanese.

After the violent battle of Saipan, the United States captured the smaller Mariana island of Tinian more easily. But another fierce assault had already begun 100 miles south, on the largest of the Mariana islands—Guam.

THE BATTLE OF GUAM

On the same day as the attack on Pearl Harbor, Japan had also captured the Pacific island of Guam. The United States had held that island since 1898 and had constructed important airfields there. Guam also had a valuable deepwater harbor, where ships could be repaired without having to travel all the way back to the United States. The capture of Guam was a serious loss for the United States.

Vaguely resembling a boot with the toes pointing downward, Guam measures only about 30 miles from top to bottom and 10 miles across. It is an island of rugged limestone and dense jungles, with only a small area of beach. On that narrow shore were many things of military importance in 1944, including the town of Agana, a navy yard, and the island's main airfield. That air base, just 1,300 miles from Tokyo, would be close enough for the United States to launch its new B-29 bombers. In addition to the island's military importance, its recapture would boost morale among both U.S. troops and civilians.

U.S. ships began a preinvasion bombardment (to soften Japanese strongholds) of Guam on July 19. Two days later, the landings began. U.S. troops waded ashore and headed inland toward Orote Peninsula, a well-fortified point that held the island's main airfield.

The Third Marine Division stormed the beach of Asan, north of Orote Peninsula.

Wartime Entertainment

While troops were fighting in Asia and Europe, Americans at home listened to songs, watched movies, and read books about the war. Writer James Jones was on Oahu when the Japanese attacked Pearl Harbor. He wrote about his experiences in *From Here to Eternity,* a best-selling novel that was later made into a Hollywood movie. Popular songs with wartime themes played on the radio. Examples included "Rosie the Riveter" (about U.S. female factory workers), "Boogie Woogie Bugle Boy," and "Don't Sit under the Apple Tree."

Movie theaters were always crowded. Before the movies, theaters showed short documentary films called newsreels, with updates about the war. Popular war movies included *Flying Tigers* (1942), starring John Wayne as a fighter pilot in China. *Thirty Seconds over Tokyo* (1944) featured Spencer Tracy and Van Johnson as participants in the Doolittle Raid. *Bataan* (1943) reproduced the Battle of the Philippines in a tense movie starring Robert Taylor.

Men of the First Provisional Marine Brigade assaulted Agat Beach, south of the peninsula. Soon afterward, another wave of marines joined the troops pushing onward to Agat.

Meanwhile, the Japanese defenders had expected the U.S. invasion and had prepared well. The ridges just beyond the two beaches were dotted with artillery. When the U.S. troops tried wading to shore, they were greeted with a hailstorm of shellfire. Some of them were hit before they even reached the beach. The first few days of the assault saw little progress, and most of the corpses

EYEWITNESS QUOTE:
THE INVASION OF GUAM

"As we landed on the beach, people were dropping right and left. There was mass confusion. We carried small shovels so that we could dig a foxhole as quickly as we could and not be seen quite so readily."

—Clyde E. Weeks Jr.,
U.S. Marine Corps

on the beaches were American.

However, by the evening of July 25, U.S. marines had captured the main road across Orote Peninsula, blocking the normal escape route from the Japanese post. Realizing their desperate situation, the Japanese commander gathered his men in a mangrove swamp near the U.S. lines. There, before attempting a frantic breakout, they drank a huge store of liquor they had been guarding along with the airfield itself.

The U.S. troops in the front lines were awakened the following night by shrill

Taking part in the invasion of Guam, two U.S. officers plant the first U.S. flag on the beach of the Japanese-held island. The men improvised quickly, raising the flag on a piece of ship mast only eight minutes into the assault.

Nurses at War

During World War II, women joined all-female units in the U.S. Army, U.S. Navy, Coast Guard, and Marine Corps. Although the U.S. government did not allow women to serve in combat, many women went through rigorous training. Some found themselves in life-threatening wartime situations.

Army nurses, for instance, took an intensive four-week training program. They went on 20-mile hikes wearing combat boots, steel helmets, and 30-pound backpacks. They learned to pitch tents, dig foxholes, purify water, and defuse bombs. They crawled on their stomachs through barbed-wire-laced trenches while dynamite exploded around them and machine-gun bullets sprayed overhead.

More than 100 army and navy nurses were serving in island hospitals when Japan captured Guam in December 1941 and the Philippines in April 1942. Together with U.S. servicemen who surrendered, these nurses were then shipped to Japanese prison camps.

U.S. nurses slide down a hill in the Burmese jungle in 1944.

voices and raucous laughter. Shortly after midnight, the giddy Japanese charged across the swamp toward the marine-held lines wielding flags, rifles, swords, pitchforks, and even empty bottles. They were too drunk to fight effectively and soon fled back toward the swamp under heavy fire.

Other Japanese units on Guam were more effective. For three weeks, U.S. Marines and U.S. Army infantry (foot soldiers) met fierce opposition as they advanced slowly. Native Chamorros, who had been treated as slaves by the Japanese, were hopeful that the Americans would free them. They hid cautiously behind U.S. lines.

The last Japanese resistance was broken, and Guam was declared a U.S. territory again on August 10. The Americans counted 1,435 men dead or missing in action out of the 55,000 troops who had fought. By comparison, nearly all of the 19,000 Japanese fighters on the island were thought to be dead, because very few of them would agree to surrender.

THE BATTLE OF
4) LEYTE GULF

With 250,000 fighting men aboard, more than 600 U.S. ships left the Marshall Islands and steamed toward Leyte Gulf in the Philippines. Stretching farther than the eye could see, the U.S. armada (large fleet) consisted of Vice Admiral Thomas C. Kinkaid's Seventh Fleet and Admiral William F. Halsey's Third Fleet, along with a few Australian ships. The date was October 14, 1944, two and a half years after General Douglas MacArthur had told the Filipino people that he would return. He was aboard one of those U.S. ships and eager to fulfill his promise.

The Japanese were prepared for Allied troops to land on the islands of Leyte Gulf, and they realized that their own situation was desperate. Operation Galvanic had already resulted in the capture of the Solomon, Mariana, Gilbert, and Marshall Islands. The Japanese could not allow the United States to reclaim the Philippines, which were even closer to their homeland. To stop the Americans, Japan developed a complicated strategy, dividing its fleet into three forces—Northern, Southern, and Central.

The Northern Force was commanded by Vice Admiral Jisaburo Ozawa. Seriously weakened by U.S. assaults, the force had only 116 aircraft remaining. The Southern Force, under the command of Vice Admiral Shoji Nishimura, was somewhat stronger. The Central Force, commanded by Vice

Admiral Takeo Kurita, was by far the most powerful of the three.

Japan's strategy relied on careful coordination of the three forces. Ozawa's weak Northern Force would serve as a decoy, or trick. Its assignment was to lure Halsey's Third Fleet away from the major scene of action in Leyte Gulf. Meanwhile, the Kurita and Nishimura forces would sail around the gulf from the north and south to attack Kinkaid's Seventh Fleet from the rear.

"I HAVE RETURNED"

The American strategy began by softening up the beaches of Leyte Gulf with air bombardment. Then the men of U.S. general Walter Krueger's Sixth Army were the first troops to land. On October 20, they began wading to shore along the coastlines of several islands in Leyte Gulf. Among them, with water up to his knees, was General Douglas MacArthur. Reaching land, he made his famous announcement to the Filipino people, saying, "I have returned."

Compared to the horrors of previous landings on Pacific islands, the invasion of the Leyte Gulf islands was relatively easy for the Americans. After nearly three years

of warfare, Japan had lost much of its infantry through battle and suicide. New replacements were young, poorly trained, and less eager to die for the emperor. Nevertheless, Japan still had some awesome warships in its navy. They included the two most powerful battleships ever built, *Yamato* and *Musashi*. Despite the easy Allied ground invasion, the Japanese were still ready for a fight.

PALAWAN PASSAGE AND THE BATTLE OF THE SIBUYAN SEA

On October 23, the U.S. submarines *Darter* and *Dace* spotted enemy ships on radar. The ships moving through the Palawan Passage belonged to Vice Admiral Kurita's Central Force.

The Japanese Central Force steams toward the Philippines to engage U.S. forces there in 1944.

After notifying Admiral Halsey of the approaching vessels, the submarines went on the attack. Firing torpedoes, the U.S. submarines sank two Japanese cruisers. One of the cruisers was *Atago,* Kurita's flagship. Kurita and his staff were rescued from the water. But others weren't so lucky. More than 300 Japanese seamen went to their doom on *Atago.* Kurita set up his new headquarters on the superbattleship *Yamato* and pushed onward toward the Sibuyan Sea.

Still before daylight on October 23, U.S. submarine *Darter* ran aground while circling the Japanese cruiser *Takao* at Palawan Passage. All *Darter's* crew transferred to *Dace* and helped try to blow up the stranded submarine before the Japanese could enter it and steal U.S. secrets. Their efforts, however, were unsuccessful. *Darter* was still perched on a shoal as a Japanese plane flew overhead. Then, with two crews crammed uncomfortably into one submarine, *Dace* headed toward safety in Australia.

The next day, Halsey's carriers launched aircraft in five separate waves, severely crippling Kurita's fleet in the Sibuyan Sea. In addition to other losses, the superbattleship *Musashi* sank to the ocean floor with more than 1,000 men aboard. *Yamato, Musashi's* twin, was also damaged. It didn't sink but struggled off to the west in the company of other ships of the Central Force.

With the Central Force seemingly crippled, Admiral Halsey turned his attention to Ozawa's weaker Northern Force. He followed Ozawa out of the gulf, without even notifying the other U.S. admirals that he was leaving. The Japanese trick had worked.

THE BATTLE OF SURIGAO STRAIT

Elsewhere, at Surigao Strait, a part of Thomas Kinkaid's Seventh Fleet was waiting to attack Nishimura's Southern Force. Because of state-of-the-art radar equipment, U.S. rear admiral Jesse B. Oldendorf knew that enemy ships were headed his

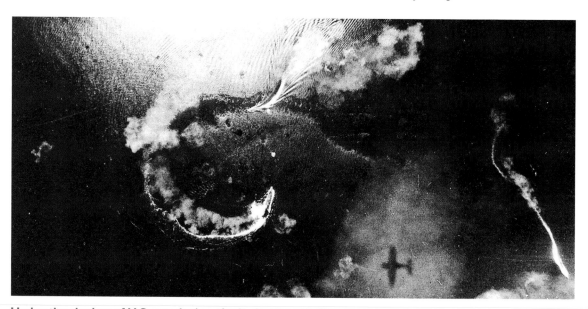

Under the shadow of U.S. attack aircraft, the Japanese battleship *Yamato (center)* maneuvers to escape falling bombs during the Battle of the Sibuyan Sea in October 1944.

way. But inferior Japanese radar had failed to pick up Oldendorf's fleet of powerful destroyers, waiting in a semicircle just outside the strait.

As the Japanese ships came through the narrow passage, Oldendorf gave the order to fire. All at once, the leading Japanese ship was attacked from every direction. The Japanese became confused. They didn't know which way to return fire. And the strait was so narrow that the ships couldn't turn around to flee. One by one, they kept coming and were sunk.

Within 20 minutes, more than 3,250 shells had hit Nishimura's vessels. His flagship, *Yamashiro*, rolled over and sank with nearly 1,200 crewmen and officers aboard. Altogether, Japanese losses included two battleships, two heavy cruisers, and three destroyers.

As news spread among the radio rooms of all the U.S. ships at Leyte Gulf, the Americans began celebrating their victory. Japan's Southern Force was wiped out. The Northern Force had left the area. And the Central Force was retreating west.

BACK FOR MORE

On the morning of October 25, Lieutenant Everett E. Roberts Jr. stood on the deck of his ship, which, by coincidence, was also named *Roberts*. Because of a typhoon (hurricane), *Samuel B. Roberts* and the rest of its unit, named Taffy 3, had been separated from other ships in the Seventh Fleet. Under the command of Rear Admiral Clifton Sprague, Taffy 3 included six small aircraft carriers (sometimes called Jeep carriers), three destroyers, and four destroyer escorts. The unit was organized only for

Yamashiro under heavy attack from U.S. aircraft during the Battle of Surigao Strait in October 1944. *Yamashiro* soon went to the bottom, taking about 1,200 officers and crew members with it.

softening up enemy beaches. Its ships were too small and too lightly armed for heavy ocean combat. After bombing the beaches, the unit was supposed to leave the Leyte Gulf area and head for safety. A day behind schedule, the unit had completed its softening-up assignment and was ready to move out of Leyte Gulf.

Lieutenant Roberts watched some tiny specks on the ocean and assumed they were ships of Kurita's Central Force as it retreated to the west. He spoke into the ship's public-address system, telling the sailors that if they looked off in the distance behind the ship, they would see the "remnants [remains] of the imperial Japanese navy."

MINORITIES IN WORLD WAR II

JAPANESE AMERICANS

After the Japanese attack on Pearl Harbor, many U.S. citizens were distrustful of anyone Japanese. They suspected that people of Japanese descent living in the United States—even those who were U.S. citizens—might be spies.

John L. DeWitt was commanding general of the Fourth Army, headquartered in San Francisco. He led a drive to move all Japanese Americans out of coastal California, Oregon, and Washington, as well as Hawaii and Arizona (areas where most Japanese Americans lived). In February 1942, President Roosevelt signed Executive Order 9066, authorizing the internment of Japanese Americans. Japanese Americans in western states were given about 10 days to sell any property they couldn't carry. Buses then took them to temporary quarters, while the government built permanent internment camps elsewhere in the country.

Altogether, about 123,000 Japanese Americans were sent to desolate camps at 10 sites throughout the country. Two-thirds of the prisoners had been born in the United States, and about half were children. Life at the camps was regimented and bleak.

Amazingly, hundreds of young men sent to the camps still signed up for the U.S. Army. Eventually, most of them became part of the all-Japanese American 442nd Regiment, which won more medals for bravery than any other unit in the war. (The regiment served in Europe, not the Pacific.) Some Japanese-speaking Americans worked as translators during the war.

AFRICAN AMERICANS

About one million African Americans served in the military during the war. Many of them suffered from harsh discrimination. For the most part, the army kept black recruits apart from white recruits during basic training. Black soldiers slept in separate barracks, ate in separate dining halls, and played in separate recreational facilities. While some African Americans were promoted to the officer ranks, they had to struggle for the same respect, authority, and privilege granted to white officers. The Red Cross even separated blood plasma (used to treat wounded soldiers) donated by black and white Americans.

Aboard U.S. ships, black enlisted men were assigned the most undesirable tasks, such as cleaning kitchens and toilets. They also worked as servants— waiting on tables, doing laundry, and shining shoes for white officers.

One notable exception was the service of 970 African Americans known as the Tuskegee Airmen. After completing pilot training at Tuskegee, Alabama, they flew more than 15,000 missions over Europe, North Africa, and the Mediterranean region between May 1943 and June 1945. They destroyed 251

Two Navajo code talkers relay information to their Allied commanders via radio using code based on the Navajo language. The code proved to be unbreakable.

enemy aircraft and received more than 850 medals. No comparable black squadron served in the Pacific, however.

NATIVE AMERICANS

Native Americans also served in the U.S. military in World War II. Many of them were Navajos, members of a large southwestern tribe. A white man named Philip Johnston, who had grown up in a Navajo community, knew that the Navajo language was very complex. Very few people spoke the language, and it had no written alphabet. Because so few people knew Navajo, Johnston suggested that the U.S. military use it as a code language.

In 1942 the Marine Corps recruited 29 Native Americans who could speak both Navajo and English. These men created a dictionary of military terms using Navajo code words. Called code talkers, Navajo speakers then sent coded military messages over telephones and radios. Altogether, about 400 Navajos worked as code talkers in the Pacific. The Japanese never broke the Navajo code.

This photograph of the destroyer USS *Samuel B. Roberts* and its defiant crew was taken one week before it engaged the Japanese Central Force off Samar Island, Philippines, in October 1944.

But to the eyes of sonar operator Whitney Felt, the specks were growing more visible. If the enemy was retreating, why were the dots getting larger? Then he saw colored smoke and heard thudding and splashing on the left side of the ship. Powerful enemy cruisers were attacking *Roberts,* a small destroyer escort equipped with only two five-inch guns. The previous night, Vice Admiral Kurita had ordered his ships to return to their previous destination in Leyte Gulf.

Kurita's entire Central Force was advancing toward U.S. Taffy 3. The force included an impressive group of four battleships, 6 heavy cruisers, 2 light cruisers, and 11 destroyers supported by land-based aircraft. Not only was Kurita's firepower far superior to Sprague's, but his cruisers and destroyers could travel nearly twice as fast as the little U.S. Jeep carriers.

In addition, many of Taffy's planes weren't immediately available. Most were off fighting other missions. And the planes the unit did have on hand had been loaded with light bombs to destroy artillery on the ground, not heavy bombs or torpedoes to damage armored warships.

Admiral Sprague feared that his little unit couldn't last 15 minutes against the fast-approaching enemy. But he decided to engage Kurita anyway. With hardly a moment's pause, he ordered his available pilots to "scramble," or to get into the air immediately.

Aboard the six Jeep carriers, crews scurried to carry out the commander's orders. Many of the planes had just returned from other missions. Some had been damaged by antiaircraft fire. But there was no time for repairs. Any planes that weren't operational were pushed into the sea to make room on flight decks for aircraft that were in better condition.

SMOKE AND SALVOS

As Japanese guns pounded the U.S. ships with salvos (many shots occurring at one time), Admiral Sprague spoke into his ship's microphone. "Make smoke," he commanded. Almost immediately, his crew released clouds of white chemical smoke from tanks. Heavy black smoke also poured from the ships' smokestacks. With those two kinds of smoke churning together, Kurita's force had difficulty seeing the U.S. ships. But still the salvos kept coming.

The U.S. situation grew perilous. Shells were splashing everywhere, and Taffy 3 was about to be boxed in. With columns of cruisers and destroyers heading toward his flanks (sides) and huge battleships steaming up between them, Sprague ordered a torpedo attack. He commanded his three destroyers to charge first, followed a few minutes later by the four weaker destroyer escorts. One of those destroyer escorts was *Samuel B. Roberts*.

In the *Roberts* combat center, Lieutenant Roberts felt his hands turn to ice. He knew that to deliver its torpedoes, Taffy 3's destroyers and destroyer escorts would have to race dangerously close to the Japanese monsters. Speeding faster than it was designed to go, *Roberts* was finally close

Heroism aboard USS *Roberts*

Aboard USS *Samuel B. Roberts*, one man refused to give up. An enemy shell landed near a gun at the back of the ship. But that didn't stop Paul Henry Carr, a gunner's mate who had previously kept the gun in shiny-as-glass condition. Under Carr's leadership, the crew worked feverishly to continue loading the gun. Straining and lifting, they used whatever ammunition they could reach. But as the men attempted to fire, the gun exploded so violently that fuse setter Sam Blue was blown unconscious into the water. The life jacket he was wearing inflated on impact, and Blue was later rescued. But that same explosion ripped Carr's body wide open from his neck to his groin. Although mortally wounded, he continued working, without realizing the seriousness of his injury or that his gun was no longer able to fire. A machinist's mate, Chalmer Goheen, found Carr trying to lift an 84-pound shell. Goheen took it away and laid his shipmate down. When Goheen came back a few minutes later, Carr had risen to his feet and was trying again to load the shell. This time, Goheen picked Carr up and carried him out to the deck, where he soon died. For his heroism, Carr received a Navy Cross (the second-highest naval honor) after his death.

enough to the enemy to deliver its three torpedoes. Captain Robert W. Copeland gave the order to fire, and off they went.

Thanks to skillful maneuvering by Captain Copeland, *Roberts* escaped serious harm for nearly two hours of the battle.

Then, while trying to avoid 14-inch shells from a distant battleship, it was suddenly hit by three 8-inch shells from a nearby cruiser. No longer able to maneuver, *Roberts* became a sitting target for the Japanese Central Force. By 9:00 A.M., nearly half the *Roberts* crew had been killed, and the ship was a hunk of twisted and blackened metal. It could no longer fight or even move. Captain Copeland gave the order to abandon ship.

> EYEWITNESS QUOTE:
> ON THE STAND OF TAFFY 3
> **"It was like bees striking at lions."**
> —**Henry A. Pyzdrowski, pilot, U.S. Navy**

With their ship dead in the water, the crew struggled to deploy flotation devices as quickly as they could. Eventually, three of the ship's four life rafts were safely launched. But they weren't big enough to hold the ship's approximately 150 surviving crew members. Most of the men were forced to remain in the water, clinging to nets attached to the rafts. (It was two days before they were rescued.)

WOMEN IN WORLD WAR II

During World War I (1914–1918), nearly 13,000 female civilians had served as clerical workers for the U.S. Navy and the U.S. Marine Corps. In 1941, 23 years later, U.S. congresswoman Edith Rogers of Massachusetts remembered those women. With war again looming, Rogers felt that women should be allowed to join the U.S. Army. She wanted Congress to establish a women's branch of the army, called the Women's Army Auxiliary Corps, or WAAC.

This U.S. government poster from World War II encourages women to serve their country by joining the military.

Although some members of Congress thought women should stay at home to do housework and care for children, others agreed with Rogers's plan. In May 1942, President Roosevelt signed a Women's Army Auxiliary Corps bill into law.

The term *auxiliary* was soon dropped, and Oveta Culp Hobby became the first director of the Women's Army Corps (WAC). Enlistees had to be over 21 years old and in good health. They held a variety of jobs—working as medical technicians, mapmakers, clerks, and secretaries, for instance—in the United

States and overseas. By the time the war ended in 1945, approximately 100,000 women had worn the WAC uniform. Other women in the army included thousands of nurses (members of the Army Nurse Corps) and more than 1,800 WASP (Women Airforce Service Pilots), who flew military aircraft to bases all over the world.

The navy also created a women's unit to free up male sailors for sea duty. Called WAVES (Women Accepted for Volunteer Emergency Service), the unit had higher standards for enlistees than did the WAC. Volunteers had to have at least two years of college experience, plus two years of professional or business experience. Led by Mildred H. McAfee, president of Wellesley College, WAVES held communications, air traffic control, navigation, and clerical jobs. Recruiting ended in 1945, with a total enrollment of 86,000 women.

This poster from World War II shows the might and determination of "Rosie the Riveter," a symbol of all working women contributing to the war effort.

SPARS (standing for Semper Paratus, Always Ready—the Coast Guard motto in Latin and then English) were female Coast Guard members. Their duties were similar to those of WAVES. SPARS enlistment reached a peak of 10,000 women by the end of the war. The last service to admit women, the U.S. Marines opened its doors to women on January 28, 1943.

Women who didn't join the military still contributed to the war effort. Because so many men were needed to fight, employers couldn't find enough men to fill jobs on the home front. Women, who had once been hired only for jobs such as teaching, nursing, and office work, became cab drivers, gas station attendants, and even factory workers. By war's end, women made up almost half the workforce in U.S. factories and shipyards. But they were paid much less than men doing the same jobs. And when the war ended, these types of jobs went to returning soldiers. Most women returned home to their traditional jobs as wives and mothers.

Then a strange event suddenly occurred. The far superior Japanese Central Force, which could have destroyed all the ships and men of Taffy 3, turned around and headed in the other direction. The Americans didn't know why, but after the war it was learned that Kurita thought he was facing a much more powerful force than his own. Believing he couldn't win, he had retreated. By fighting so valiantly, the little ships of Taffy 3 had fooled the Japanese into retreating. "By the skillful use of smoke, the launching of daring torpedo attacks, and the refusal to break off action in the face of overwhelming odds and sure losses, this intrepid little group of fighting ships accomplished one of the most heroic and gallant epics of the war," wrote Vice Admiral Kinkaid afterward.

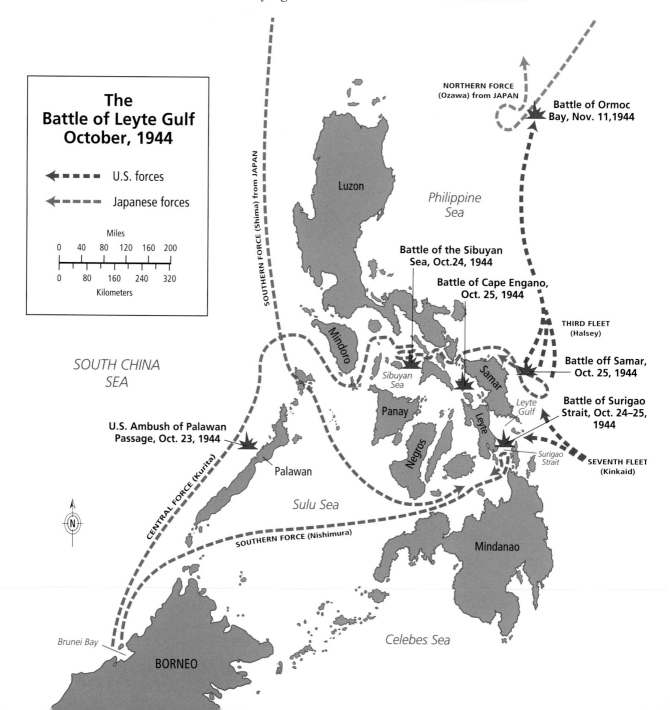

The Battle of Leyte Gulf October, 1944

◄ ─ ─ ─ U.S. forces

◄ ─ ─ ─ Japanese forces

Miles
0   40   80   120   160   200

0   80   160   240   320
Kilometers

SOUTHERN FORCE (Shima) from JAPAN

NORTHERN FORCE (Ozawa) from JAPAN

Battle of Ormoc Bay, Nov. 11, 1944

Luzon

Philippine Sea

Battle of the Sibuyan Sea, Oct. 24, 1944

Battle of Cape Engano, Oct. 25, 1944

THIRD FLEET (Halsey)

Mindoro

SOUTH CHINA SEA

Sibuyan Sea

Samar

Battle off Samar, Oct. 25, 1944

Panay

Leyte Gulf

Battle of Surigao Strait, Oct. 24–25, 1944

U.S. Ambush of Palawan Passage, Oct. 23, 1944

CENTRAL FORCE (Kurita)

Palawan

Negros

Leyte

Surigao Strait

SEVENTH FLEET (Kinkaid)

Sulu Sea

SOUTHERN FORCE (Nishimura)

N

Mindanao

Brunei Bay

Celebes Sea

BORNEO

Japan's "Divine Wind"

The word *kamikaze* means "divine wind" in Japanese and refers to a sacred event in Japanese history. In 1281 a huge Mongol fleet commanded by Kublai Khan attempted to invade Japan. When the greatly outnumbered Japanese prayed for a miracle, a typhoon (hurricane) arrived, destroying hundreds of enemy ships and saving the island nation. The typhoon was therefore considered a divine wind.

As 1944 drew to a close, the Japanese feared that they were losing the war. Desperate to hang on to the Philippines, Japanese admirals met on October 19 to discuss new strategies. Admiral Takijiro Onishi suggested a radical idea called kamikaze missions. Pilots would deliberately crash their planes into enemy vessels, killing themselves in the process.

Before that time, pilots on both sides sometimes chose to crash into enemy targets. Knowing that their damaged planes would go down anyway, they headed full speed toward enemy ships instead of simply falling into the sea. But suicide flights became an official tactic among the Japanese admirals at the Battle of Leyte Gulf.

A kamikaze pilot is shot down before he can fly his plane into USS *Kitkin Bay* in 1944. Another kamikaze pilot was later more successful, striking and damaging *Kitkin Bay*.

Yet Japanese pilots had by then taken to the skies. On that day, October 25, suicide airplane attacks, called kamikaze attacks, became an official tactic of the Japanese navy. As Kurita's fleet turned away, kamikaze pilots appeared overhead. Ordered to crash into American ships, they headed straight for the Jeep carriers of Taffy 3. One crash damaged *Kitkin Bay*. Another barely missed *White Plains*. A third also missed *White Plains* but struck *Saint Lo* instead, causing an explosion that sank the little Jeep carrier. *Saint Lo* thus became acknowledged as the first ship sunk by a kamikaze plane.

The Battle of Leyte Gulf ended on October 26, 1944, after only three days of combat. With it, the Allies were able to retake the Philippines. And the Japanese had not only failed to prevent the Allied landing but had lost 300,000 tons of warships in the process. The crippled Japanese navy was no longer a serious threat in the Pacific.

THE FINAL PUSH

5

Despite losing the Philippines, the Japanese people were far from willing to accept defeat. To make the Japanese surrender, the Americans needed to establish an air base close enough to attack the Japanese homeland. The next stepping-stone was the island of Iwo Jima, only 550 miles from Tokyo.

Resembling a burned pork chop from above, the little volcanic island was eyed jealously by Americans as they piloted B-29 Superfortress bombers from Saipan toward Tokyo. Although the island measured less than five by three miles, the United States had several reasons for wanting Iwo Jima. It housed two completed airfields, plus another one under construction. If the United States could capture the island, those fields could provide emergency land-ing areas for U.S. planes. Also, the island was equipped with rare Japanese radar equipment, which allowed men on the ground to notify Tokyo when enemy aircraft were approaching. The Americans wanted to stop those transmissions. But most important the United States wanted Iwo Jima in order to control air bases so close to the Japanese homeland.

ISLAND FORTIFICATIONS

The Japanese High Command was fully aware of the island's importance and sent one of the nation's most able generals to command it. He was Lieutenant General Tadamichi Kuribayashi, a 54-year-old veteran of the China campaign and a former commander of the emperor's elite Imperial Guard.

Standing five feet nine inches tall and weighing 200 pounds, Kuribayashi was unimpressive in appearance. But he was a skilled strategist who was as realistic as he was determined. Like Admiral Yamamoto, he had spent time in Washington, D.C., and had developed a healthy respect for U.S. industrial power. Like Yamamoto, he had been outspoken in his criticism of a war with the United States. But he placed his duty to the empire above all else and accepted his military assignments with courage and skill.

Convinced that U.S. troops would ultimately capture Iwo Jima, Kuribayashi wanted to hold off the capture as long as possible—and with maximum casualties to the enemy. On reaching the island, he put his troops to work digging an underground fortification of caves and con-

Tokyo Rose

Throughout the war, the Japanese government made daily radio broadcasts to demoralize (weaken the spirits of) U.S. troops in the Pacific. Between recordings of American popular music, a woman the Americans called Tokyo Rose spoke English in a sultry voice. She reported fake U.S. casualty figures and told the men that their wives and sweethearts at home were being unfaithful.

crete pillboxes. To connect them, he planned a spidery network of reinforced tunnels. By the time the Americans reached Iwo Jima in February 1945, the Japanese had constructed hundreds of hidden pillboxes.

The coastal waters around Iwo Jima teem with U.S. landing craft during the first wave of the U.S. assault on the strategic island in February 1945.

Marines inch their way through volcanic soil and Japanese defensive fire during the invasion of Iwo Jima on February 19, 1945.

The walls of each pillbox were made of reinforced concrete measuring 8 feet thick. On top was a 50-foot layer of black Iwo Jima earth. One of the underground structures went down several levels, providing space for hospital care and storage as well as troop protection during bomb and mortar attacks.

Under Kuribayashi's supervision, tiny Iwo Jima became the best-fortified island in the Pacific. Except for the airfields, it was also the best camouflaged (protected by disguise). Furthermore, Kuribayashi's troops were extremely determined to punish anyone who might try to steal their territory. The general had delivered a stern order to his troops, saying it was the duty of every man to kill 10 of the enemy before dying himself.

THE U.S. INVASION

Admiral Nimitz had assigned Vice Admiral Raymond A. Spruance to command the overall assault on Iwo Jima. Spruance's Fifth Fleet would also take part in the pre-invasion bombardment of the island by sea and air. Rear Admiral Richmond Turner

and Major General Harry Schmidt would supervise the amphibious (sea-to-shore) landings.

On February 19, 1945, after three weeks of preinvasion attacks, great waves of marines churned toward shore in hundreds of landing craft. Veterans of previous Pacific island landings, they expected to be greeted with crazed banzai attacks or at least heavy artillery fire. But the Japanese guns were silent. The only shells came from the U.S. ships behind the marines and arced well over their heads.

Briefly, the Americans wondered if the island had been deserted. But Kuribayashi had told his men to hold their fire. He knew the Americans would soon be a frantic confusion of men and machines in the knee-deep volcanic ash that lined the island's shores. Then the Japanese could attack. And the U.S. warships would stop firing to avoid hitting their own men.

"WAR IS HELL"

As thousands of Americans slipped and stumbled onto the beaches, Kuribayashi ordered his men to fire. Ear-splitting barrages came from every direction. Marine captain Lawrence Cracroft, a combat veteran, was among the U.S. troops at Iwo Jima. Years later, he recalled the inferno:

> Artillery shells and mortar rounds whistled and swished over us, and the nearer their explosions the greater our terror. The closest rounds added the screams of the victims to the night's horrors. . . . The night's most dreadful noises were created by Japanese weapons of which we had no prior knowledge, a 320mm spigot mortar and huge rockets. The sounds of [the missiles] in transit were horrifying.
>
> Inevitably some rockets and mortar rounds hit gasoline fueled vehicles and ammunition stockpiles and the resulting [explosions and raging fires] added to the night's general hell.

Rifle and bayonet thrust forward, a fallen marine maintains a battle position even in death on the sands of Iwo Jima, February 19, 1945. The U.S. invasion fleet is visible behind him.

Risking death, a marine sticks his head above a dune to pinpoint a Japanese machine-gun nest, while his buddies locate the position on a map of Iwo Jima during the U.S. advance across the island in February 1945. Moments later, the men radio the information to artillery units for precise shelling of the location.

But the Americans hung on. General Schmidt divided the U.S. troops into separate units to capture the airfields and Mount Suribachi, the island's main peak. Then the troops would rejoin one another to drive north. By February 23, the fourth day of fighting, marines had clawed their way up the slopes of Mount Suribachi. There, on the top of the inactive volcano, a patrol under Lieutenant Harold Schrier raised a small U.S. flag measuring 54 by 28 inches. Schrier soon got a much larger flag from a landing ship and ordered six of his men to raise it on a much longer pole. (Photographer Joe Rosenthal captured the scene, *facing page,* which quickly became one of the most famous images of World War II.)

Fighting on the island was bloody and desperate. But in the end, American equipment proved to be superior. The Americans fought with tanks outfitted with flamethrowers, which spewed burning liquid into Japanese pillboxes and tunnels. Eventually, U.S. forces overran the Japanese fortifications.

On March 25, 1945, Iwo Jima was officially declared a U.S.-captured territory.

EYEWITNESS QUOTE:
FLAG RAISING, IWO JIMA

"When we got there . . . the Lieutenant sent a man around to look for a piece of staff [flagpole] that we could put the American flag on. And the [Japanese] had some old pipes that were laying around there. . . . And we used this . . . pipe and we attached the American flag on there and we put it up."

—John H. Bradley, pharmacist's mate, U.S. Navy

However, that night a group of Japanese soldiers charged from behind crevices and rocks for one last desperate attack on the sleeping Americans. But their cause was hopeless. By morning 223 Japanese warriors lay dead. One of them was General Kuribayashi. Historians disagree about Kuribayashi's death. Some say he committed suicide that night. Others say he died in battle, fighting to the end alongside ordinary Japanese soldiers.

One thing is certain. The U.S. Marine Corps paid dearly for victory, suffering its highest casualty rate up to that point in history. About 25,000 marines—30 percent of the landing force—were killed or wounded in the campaign. More than 20 marines earned the Medal of Honor (the nation's highest award) for their achievements at Iwo Jima.

NEXT STOP: OKINAWA

Lying 340 miles south of mainland Japan, Okinawa is a narrow coral island in the Ryukyu chain. It is about 70 miles long and 18 miles across at its widest point.

A Classic Photo

Joe Rosenthal, an Associated Press photographer, was with the U.S. forces installing the flag on Mount Suribachi on Iwo Jima. He snapped a picture of the men as they struggled to force the flagpole into the volcanic earth. The photograph has been reproduced in thousands of publications, on posters, and on stamps. It has become the most famous symbol of U.S. victory in World War II.

Many people seeing the photograph assume the flag was raised when the U.S. Marines finally captured Iwo Jima from the Japanese. However, the picture was taken on only the fourth day of a battle that continued for another month.

The photograph portrays six marines. In the front row, left to right, are Ira Hayes, Franklin Sousley, John Bradley, and Harlon Block. Unseen behind them are their leader, Sergeant Michael Strank, and Rene Gagnon. Of the six, Strank, Block, and Sousley were killed by the time the ferocious battle ended on March 25, 1945.

MEDICAL CARE IN WORLD WAR II

The U.S. military in World War II needed a large medical system to care for wounded and sick troops. Ideally, treatment of wounded soldiers began at the front lines, beginning with army or navy medics, sometimes called corpsmen. Medics were trained in first aid and emergency medical treatment. Their work required a special kind of courage. Medics shared the same sights, smells, dangers, and fears of battle as combat troops, but they seldom carried weapons for protection. Knowing that speed saved lives, they rushed out of foxholes to aid wounded men as enemy mortars whistled, shrieked, and exploded within feet of them.

Their tools consisted of tourniquets (tight bandages) to stop bleeding, blood plasma to control shock, and sulfa (an antibiotic) to prevent infection. Medics could also give injections of morphine to relieve pain, but they were not trained to perform surgery. Burns were among the most frequent injuries they saw, and medics treated them with Vaseline covered by bandages.

After a medic gave first aid, he tagged the victim's jacket with a diagnosis. If the wounded man couldn't walk on his own, four other soldiers carried him on a stretcher to an aid station, where a doctor was on duty. Such a station might be only a foxhole or a shell crater protected by tarps and sandbags. Near the front lines, these stations were constantly at risk from enemy fire.

A U.S. Army doctor tends to a wounded soldier at an aid station in the South Pacific.

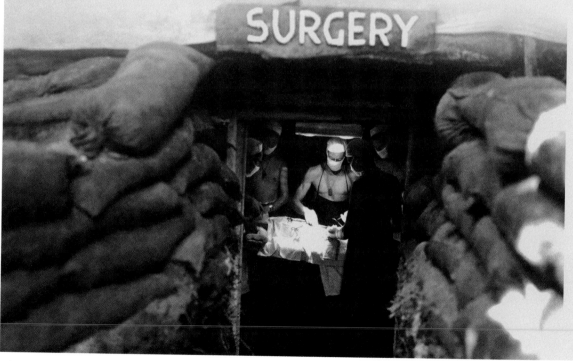

After treatment at an aid station, an injured man in the Pacific might be transported to the beach in a motorized vehicle, such as a Jeep. Like the aid stations, the vehicles were often under fire, and wounded men sometimes received additional injuries while being transported.

Once at the beach, the injured man was placed in a landing craft that took him offshore to a hospital ship waiting in the harbor. Hoisting a stretcher up to the ship was sometimes the riskiest part of the entire procedure. Waves as high as 10 feet could bounce a landing craft up and down like a Ping-Pong ball. A sudden swell could pound the stretcher furiously against the side of the ship.

Hospital ships were usually anchored 20 miles offshore. Their operating rooms were used 24 hours a day by rotating staffs of approximately 20 doctors, 40

A wounded sailor is transported from **USS** *Bunker Hill* **to another ship. Later, with others, the man will go to a hospital ship, and then to a land-based medical center.**

female nurses, and 200 corpsmen. Most ships were overcrowded, with patients lying on bare mattresses in passageways as well as on bunks. But by taking advantage of every possible bit of space, the ships could hold 600 or more patients. When fully loaded, hospital ships would sail to more fully equipped medical facilities, sometimes as far away as Australia.

Although they were painted with bright red crosses—symbols that they were medical ships, not combat vessels—hospital ships were not free from attack. For instance, on April 28, 1945, six army nurses and one navy nurse died aboard USS *Comfort* when it was struck by a suicide plane off the coast of Okinawa.

In the spring of 1945, it was the last Japanese stronghold in the Pacific. U.S. leaders considered the island, which was home to several fine airfields and harbors, to be vitally important to their invasion of Japan.

For those same reasons, the Japanese were just as desperate to hold on to the little island. They had psychological reasons, too. An invasion of Okinawa would be almost like an invasion of Japan itself. Many native Okinawans were descendants of settlers

R and R in the Pacific

World War II lasted three and a half years in the Pacific—from December 1941 until August 1945. No serviceman fought that entire time, however. Recesses from battle could last for days, weeks, or even months. Some men sketched landscapes or people. Some kept daily journals. Others wrote poetry. Nearly everyone listened to radio reports about how the war was going in Europe. Where a level playing field could be found (even on ships), service-men often split up into teams for baseball or basketball games *(right)*. More commonly, they simply played cards.

During one lull in combat, pilot Stephen Stanford was based on the tiny island of Biak, just northeast of Australia. Bored with the barren view outside his window, he sent a letter home asking for some flower seeds. His mother mailed him some hollyhock seeds, which he planted outside his barracks. Stanford was transferred soon afterward, but when he returned to Biak later, he found colorful flowers blooming where he had planted them.

The men also made time for fun onboard ship. In 1944 a convoy (group) of about 60 ships was traveling from Hawaii to Manus in the Admiralty Islands. Manus is just south of the equator. According to navy tradition, any sailor who had never crossed the equator was called a "pollywog." Men crossing for the first time went through an initiation ceremony that ranged from embarrassing (following silly orders) to downright painful (undergoing a paddling). Afterward, the men received certificates declaring them to be "shellbacks" (veteran sailors).

Most ships in the Manus convoy had not come across the Japanese for several months. But the possibility of suddenly meeting the enemy was very real. Officers wondered if it would be wise to allow the men to leave their stations to participate in mindless high jinks. Yet navy tradition was important too.

The skippers of all 60 vessels faced that same choice. At last, they agreed to allow crews of some ships to conduct initiations for a few hours while other ships watched for the enemy. Then the ships would switch, so that everyone had a turn. Even Captain Robert Copeland of USS *Samuel B. Roberts* went though the initiation ceremony that day.

The massive invasion force at Okinawa, Japan, in April 1945. Landing craft of many kinds bring men and supplies ashore at the beachhead (secured area), while destroyers and cruisers *(far background)* protect the landing operation from seaborne attack.

who had arrived from Japan hundreds of years earlier, bringing Japanese culture, belief systems, and religion with them. The two island nations shared a strong bond.

A HUGE AND COMPLICATED LANDING

The invasion of Okinawa, which began on April 1, 1945, was to be the largest fleet movement in U.S. history. Marine second lieutenant Jeptha J. Carrell was new to combat when he took part in the invasion. Fifty years later, he still remembered the U.S. forces as "awesome."

"The impression of power was not merely reassuring," Carrell reported in a 1994 memoir. "It was almost unbelievable. Over a half million men and 1,457 ships participated.

There were 530 troopships. Twenty-five ships carried nothing but Jeeps. The submarine fleet alone totaled over 50 vessels. Combat surface vessels included over 40 carriers, 18 battleships, scores of cruisers, and nearly 150 destroyers and destroyer escorts."

Sixty thousand U.S. troops participated in the first wave of the attack, and that was only a fraction of the men who would land on Okinawa that day. Carrying their weapons, ammunition, and packs, the men also wore inflatable life preservers as they climbed down the nets lining the sides of their troopships. At the bottom of the nets, they leaped into waiting landing craft that carried them approximately 12 miles. Two miles from shore, they climbed into amphibious tractors that traveled right onto the beach.

Kamikazes over Okinawa

By the time of the Battle of Okinawa, most highly skilled Japanese pilots had already died in the war, and new young pilots were poorly trained. They wouldn't have stood a chance in a contest against veteran U.S. pilots in their state-of-the-art Hellcat fighter planes. But by then, most new Japanese pilots were sent out as kamikazes. They didn't need skill or experience to crash into an enemy target—they just needed courage. By volunteering to die for their country, they hoped to become war heroes and to bring honor to their families.

Kamikaze airmen wore special ceremonial clothing. These included headbands with Japan's red and white Rising Sun symbol, white silk scarves, and "thousand stitch belts." The mother of each pilot honorably gathered 1,000 stitches from Japanese citizens (or stitched them herself) to create this special belt, symbolizing the love, hope, and pride of his family and community.

When the pilot received orders for his suicide mission, a special ritual began. The evening before his flight, he gave away all his personal possessions. The next morning, he arose before dawn, washed carefully, and put on a clean uniform. At the airfield, he and other kamikaze pilots sat at long tables to drink rice wine from ceremonial bowls. Then they shouted "banzai" and boarded their flying tombs.

Most kamikaze pilots failed to hit anything that would cause an explosion, such as a ship's fuel tank. As a result, not all of them caused serious harm to their targets. They were, however, very successful in sacrificing themselves. More than 3,000 Japanese pilots died this way.

Defending Okinawa was Japan's Thirty-second Army, consisting of 130,000 men (including about 20,000 Okinawans). Their commander was Lieutenant General Mitsuru Ushijima. With limited numbers of troops and weapons, he concentrated his forces on the southern end of Okinawa, in the interior of the island. To save ammunition, he planned to let the Americans land before ordering his troops to fire. Like General Kuribayashi at Iwo Jima, Ushijima knew his cause was doomed. But he told his men to kill as many Americans as possible before dying themselves.

L STANDS FOR *Love*

Under the command of U.S. Army lieutenant general Simon Bolivar Buckner, the first wave of attackers splashed ashore. Fearing a violent battle like the one at Iwo Jima, the men moved cautiously. But very little happened. There were no deafening mortar bursts and hardly any rifle fire. Out of more than 100,000 Americans who landed, only 25 died that first day. The situation was so calm that the troops began joking that L Day (for "Landing Day") really stood for "Love Day."

Army troops headed south, toward fortified hills and ancient aboveground tombs. Marine troops headed north. Pressing forward, they reached the main airfield and claimed it by noon. For almost a week, the Americans continued on their journeys, encountering almost no resistance. Then, on day five, General Ushijima finally gave the signal to fire. From the hundreds of natural and human-made caves that honeycombed the island came the thunder of heavy artillery. In some instances, the defenders waited until Americans had struggled over crests of hills and then shot them in the back.

On the sixth day came the howl of "divine wind," the Japanese term for their suicide flights. Kamikaze planes rained down in fiery explosions on U.S. tanks, guns, and troops below. In the Battle of Leyte Gulf, when kamikaze flights had first become an official tactic, only a handful of Japanese pilots had volunteered for suicide missions. Six months later, at Okinawa, thousands of young men wanted the job.

Over Okinawa, kamikaze pilots filled the sky. Despite antiaircraft fire, several of them reached U.S. aircraft carriers offshore. Admiral Marc Mitscher commanded Task Force 58, which included all U.S. carriers in the battle. He was in Okinawa Harbor on his beautiful new flagship *Bunker Hill* when a suicide pilot struck. Crashing into the planes on the carrier's flight deck, the kamikaze triggered a series of explosions. A second kamikaze found the same target, creating still greater horror. The two attacks left 373 Americans dead and 264 wounded.

As flames scorched the air, the crews of nearby ships rushed for hoses and pumps. They drenched *Bunker Hill* with so many tons of seawater that the carrier began to list. Mitscher and his staff quickly transferred to *Enterprise,* but another kamikaze found that ship too, killing 14 additional

The exploding and burning deck of **USS** *Bunker Hill* following a kamikaze attack in 1945

men. In all, 21 U.S. ships were sunk, and 66 were damaged, some too seriously to be repaired.

The struggle for Okinawa was a three-month inferno for both the Japanese and the Americans. Historians place American casualties during the savage fighting at 35 percent (some units lost 88 percent of their men). Not until the end of June 1945 did the Americans capture the little island. From then on, the Japanese had no other soil to defend except their home islands.

WAR'S END

6

Franklin Delano Roosevelt was inaugurated (sworn in) for a fourth term as president of the United States on January 20, 1945. He was the first U.S. president ever to serve more than two terms. Taking the oath of office as vice president that day was Harry S. Truman, a former U.S. senator from Missouri. Truman was only two years younger than the president, but he seemed much more robust. Roosevelt had caught polio 20 years earlier and was seriously crippled. But much of the U.S. public weren't aware of it. Photographers were strongly discouraged from taking pictures of the president seated in a wheelchair.

Forty-eight hours after the inauguration ceremony, Roosevelt left for an important conference at Yalta, a port city in the Soviet Union. Meeting with him were two other heads of state, Winston Churchill of Great Britain and Joseph Stalin of the Soviet Union. By then in poor health, Roosevelt died on April 12, 1945, shortly after he returned from Yalta. Harry Truman took over as president.

The day after Truman was sworn in as president, he learned about a top-secret U.S. government program called the Manhattan Project. That was the code name for the

TRUMAN TAKES OVER

On April 12, 1945, Vice President Harry Truman learned of President Roosevelt's death. He asked Mrs. Roosevelt, "Is there anything I can do for you?"

"Is there anything we can do for you?" she replied. "For you are the one in trouble now."

development of the first atomic bomb—at that time, the most powerful and deadly bomb ever made. U.S. scientists had been working day and night at laboratories in many sites across the United States and Canada. They were racing to produce an atomic weapon before the Germans did.

On May 7, 1945, less than a month after Truman became president, Germany surrendered to the Allies, ending World War II in Europe. But the war against Japan was still raging in the Pacific. During the fighting on Okinawa alone, 12,520 U.S. troops were reported killed or missing. Another 36,631 had been wounded. If U.S. soldiers had to fight on Japanese soil, their casualties would likely be far worse. That was a risk no one wanted to take.

A CRUCIAL DECISION

Trinity, the code name for the atomic bomb test, was set for July 16, 1945, near Alamogordo in southern New Mexico.

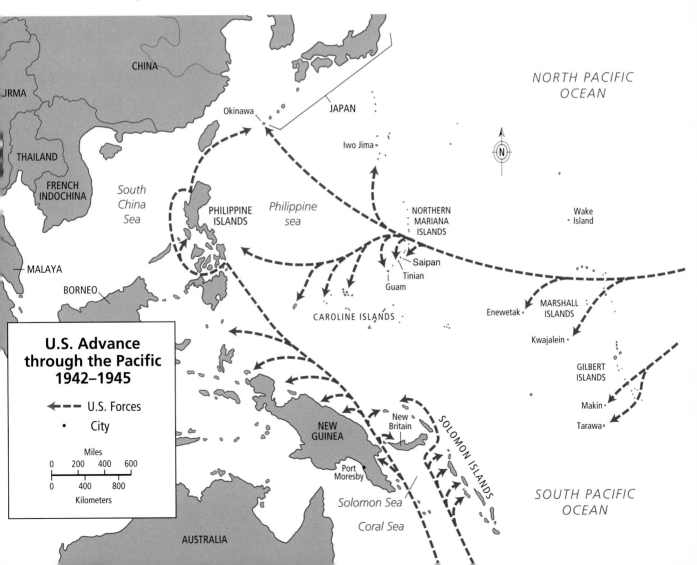

U.S. Advance through the Pacific 1942–1945

Supervised by Manhattan Project director General Leslie R. Groves, everything was handled in strict secrecy. The test was delayed an hour and a half by the possibility of rain, but the explosion finally took place at 5:29 A.M.

Witnesses reported that the desert turned brighter than any light ever seen on earth before. Then a great ball of fire rose up and up, changing colors from deep purple to orange. People as far as 250 miles away saw the brilliant flash and heard the explosion. Afterward, General Groves's secretary sent a coded message, telling President Truman that Trinity had been a success. The message reached him at sea as he was returning from Potsdam, Germany, where he had been meeting with Churchill and Stalin.

Once it was shown that an atomic bomb could be successful, Truman had to decide whether or not to use the terrible weapon against Japan. He was surrounded by advisers with many different opinions. Everyone knew the bomb would cause thousands of civilian deaths, plus horrible devastation to Japanese cities. Even some of the scientists who had helped develop the bomb were opposed to using it. But the bomb, many reasoned, would also bring about an earlier end to the conflict than warfare with battles on land and other conventional methods.

J. Robert Oppenheimer

Dr. J. Robert Oppenheimer, who directed the Manhattan Project research station at Los Alamos, New Mexico, was not only a brilliant physicist. He also spoke half a dozen foreign languages and was familiar with Asian poetry and philosophy. After graduating from Harvard in 1925, he studied at Cambridge University in England and received a Ph.D. from the University of Gottingen in Germany.

Oppenheimer had mixed feelings about the atomic bomb. Aware that Germany was working on its own atomic bomb, he felt that the United States had to produce one before the Germans did. But he hoped the United States would never use the bomb. It is rumored that he wept when the second atomic bomb was dropped on Japan (at Nagasaki).

After the war, Oppenheimer became chairman of the U.S. Atomic Energy Commission, a government agency that oversaw the development and use of nuclear (atomic) power. He fought against his old friend Edward Teller, another former Manhattan Project scientist, who wanted to develop an even more powerful bomb, a hydrogen bomb. The U.S. government accused Oppenheimer of being disloyal because of his opposition to the hydrogen bomb and his past associations with political groups opposed by the U.S. government. He lost his job but then accepted a job at Princeton University.

The awesome fireball of the Trinity atomic bomb test consumes the New Mexico desert in 1945. The success of the test was an important factor in President Truman's decision to use the new weapon in the South Pacific.

American leaders believed the bomb would save the lives of many thousands of U.S. troops. So after discussions with high-level military, political, and scientific leaders, President Truman gave the order to drop it.

ATOMIC DESTRUCTION

On August 6, 1945, three U.S. B-29s flew toward the Japanese city of Hiroshima. One of the aircraft, *Enola Gay* (named for the mother of the pilot, Colonel Paul Tibbets), carried an atomic bomb. Reaching the city, the crews released the bomb, nicknamed Little Boy, over a city that was going about its usual business. When the bomb detonated, 80 percent of Hiroshima's buildings were flattened immediately, and at least 70,000 people died instantly. But that estimate is probably low and does not include the thousands of victims who later suffered slow and agonizing deaths from radiation (a byproduct of an atomic blast often lethal to humans), severe burns, and other wounds.

The gate of a shrine in Nagasaki, Japan, remains standing amid the rubble of the city following the U.S. detonation of the atomic bomb Fat Man above the city on August 9, 1945. The bomb's destructive power led Japanese leadership to conclude the war was lost.

Amazingly, the Japanese High Command didn't respond immediately to the devastation. Japanese leaders not only refused to surrender but also withheld news of the Hiroshima bombing so that the Japanese public didn't learn full details right away.

So the Americans struck again. On August 9, a second B-29, this one named *Bock's Car,* dropped an atomic bomb nicknamed Fat Man on the Japanese city of Nagasaki. Nearly 100,000 people were killed or maimed by the blast itself or the fires it caused.

The second bomb convinced the Japanese that their fight was hopeless. On August 14, 1945, Japan agreed to surrender. News that the war was finally over created jubilation in Allied nations.

Allied military officials look on as Japanese foreign minister Mamoru Shigemutu *(seated)* signs surrender documents aboard USS *Missouri* on September 2, 1945.

In the United States, V-J Day (Victory over Japan Day) was boisterous and exciting. Horns blared, radios boomed, banners waved, and fireworks exploded. Strangers danced with each other and kissed openly in the streets.

While Americans celebrated their victory, an unparalleled gloom descended on the Japanese people. In its long history, their nation had never lost a war. Most Japanese citizens had never even considered that they might lose this one. Almost immediately after the surrender,

EYEWITNESS QUOTE:
ON SERVICE WITH HEROES

"There are so many tragedies in intensive and prolonged fighting . . . that one would think there can be no conceivable satisfaction connected with it. There is one. . . . It was simply an honor and privilege to serve with the men in my platoon."

—Jeptha J. Carrell, captain, U.S. Marine Corps

Japanese soldiers began to commit suicide. Believing they had disgraced themselves, their families, and their emperor, hundreds of officers and fighting men chose to end their anguish with death.

Nevertheless, on Sunday, September 2, nine Japanese civilian and military leaders arrived at USS *Missouri*, which was anchored in Tokyo Bay. There, with General Douglas MacArthur representing the United States and hundreds of Allied officers looking on, they signed surrender documents.

Military Awards Presented during World War II

- Medal of Honor (Congressional Medal of Honor)—the nation's highest award. Presented to members of the armed forces who risk their lives to perform outstanding acts of bravery.
- Distinguished Service Cross (awarded to members of the army or air force) and Navy Cross (awarded to members of the navy)—the second highest military decorations. Presented to members of the armed forces who perform outstanding acts of bravery.
- Silver Star—presented for gallantry
- Legion of Merit—presented for outstanding service to soldiers of friendly nations as well as members of the U.S. armed forces
- Distinguished Flying Cross—presented to persons both in and out of the military who perform acts of heroism while flying
- Bronze Star—presented for acts of heroism of a lesser degree than required for the Silver Star
- Purple Heart—presented to members of the armed services who are wounded in action

EPILOGUE

In the United States, families hoped to welcome home their husbands, brothers, and sons right away. Many young women planned to marry their returning boyfriends. But it took more than a year for all the troops to be discharged (officially released from the

military). And the veterans straggled home to encounter unexpected difficulties.

Housing construction had stopped during the war, and many veterans couldn't find apartments or houses. As a result, many men had to delay their wedding plans or move in with their parents after the war. Some men who moved back home no longer wanted to pay attention to their parents' rules or advice. Some were so hardened by war that they no longer seemed to have anything in common with their wives, sweethearts, or families.

The U.S. government tried to help the veterans readjust to civilian life. The Montgomery GI Bill, approved by Congress in 1944, paid for up to 36 months of college tuition for former servicemen with high school educations. The bill also gave veterans preferential treatment (highest priority) when they applied for housing loans or government jobs.

For some women, the end of the war brought unwelcome changes. Many women, employed by weapons factories and other workplaces during the war, had earned a salary for the first time. They resented giving up their jobs to returning soldiers. But most had no choice. Despite women's major contributions as war workers and even soldiers, most went back to traditional jobs as wives and mothers.

NEW BEGINNINGS

Under terms of the surrender agreement, the U.S. Army occupied, or took charge of, Japan. General MacArthur led the occupying forces.

Life after Internment

Outraged by the imprisonment of law-abiding citizens, several groups of Japanese and non-Japanese Americans fought to shut down the U.S. internment camps during World War II. In January 1945, seven months before the end of the war, pressure from these citizens seemed to prevail and most camps were closed. Detainees were free to leave the camps. But many had lost their homes and businesses during internment. They had to rebuild their lives from scratch, often moving, like the men at right, to U.S. regions and cities unfamiliar to them.

Despite the nation's fears, not one instance of sabotage or spying on the part of a Japanese American was ever documented. After the war, many U.S. citizens criticized the government for the internment of Japanese Americans. Years later, in a rare public criticism of President Roosevelt, President Harry Truman told the press that placing American citizens in internment camps had been wrong. Even later, in 1990, the U.S. government officially apologized to Japanese Americans. It paid $20,000 to each camp survivor as compensation for suffering and losses. To access primary source documents relating to internment, visit the Japanese American Relocation Digital Archives at <http://jarda.cdlib.org/historical_context.html>.

The United States enacted a series of economic and political reforms in Japan, designed to turn the nation into a democratic society. Under Allied leadership, Japan held its first democratic election in 1946. Almost 3,000 people ran for the 466 seats in the Japanese diet, or legislature. Candidates included 38 women, who until that time had not even been allowed to vote in Japan. Helping the cause of democracy was Emperor Hirohito's admission in 1946 that he was not descended from the sun goddess but was an ordinary mortal like all other Japanese people.

Truman's Decision

In 1956 a young political science professor asked former president Truman if it had been difficult to decide to use the atomic bomb. "No," Truman replied. "I did it to save the lives of thousands of American servicemen. I have never regretted my decision." Speaking on television in 1965, Truman repeated that statement. Mentioning estimates of 750,000 Americans who would have been killed or maimed in an invasion of Japan, he again said that he felt his decision had been right

U.S. observers oversee the first democratic elections in Japan on April 16, 1946. The United States occupied Japan until 1951, ensuring that Japanese leadership complied with surrender terms.

The United States also helped Japan adopt a democratic constitution, which went into effect in May 1947. The constitution reorganized the nation's court system, limited the power of landowners, and limited Japan's ability to rearm for war.

The United States also tried 28 top Japanese military leaders as war criminals. They were charged with "crimes against peace" for leading their nation into war. Seven of them were convicted and hanged to death on December 23, 1948. The others went to prison. An additional 5,000 Japanese were convicted of lesser crimes, such as mistreating prisoners of war. Some of them were also executed.

While the defeated Japanese struggled to rebuild their nation, the victorious United States was filled with pride and hope for the future. On V-J Day (August 14, 1945), thousands of Americans celebrated in Lafayette Park, across the street from the White House. President Truman appeared on a White House balcony to address the crowd and deliver the good news. His words summed up the relief, the joy, and the optimism of the nation as it entered a new peacetime era: "This is a great day, the day we've been waiting for. This is the day for free governments in the world. We will need the help of all of you. And I know we will get it."

Major Battles of World War II in the Pacific

Japanese attack on Pearl Harbor	December 7, 1941
Battle for Wake Island	December 8–23, 1941
Battles of Bataan and Corregidor	March–April 1942
Battle of the Coral Sea	May 4–8, 1942
Battle of Midway	June 4–7, 1942
Battles of Tulagi and Guadalcanal	August 1942–February 1943
Battle of Bloody Ridge, Solomon Islands	September 12–14, 1942
Naval Battle of Guadalcanal	November 12–15, 1942
Battles for Gilbert Islands	November 20–25, 1943
Battle of the Marshall Islands	February 1944
Battle of Saipan	June–July 1944
Battles of Tinian and Guam	July–August 1944
Battle of Leyte Gulf	October 23–26, 1944
Battle of Iowa Jima	February 19–March 26, 1945
Battle of Okinawa	April–June 1945

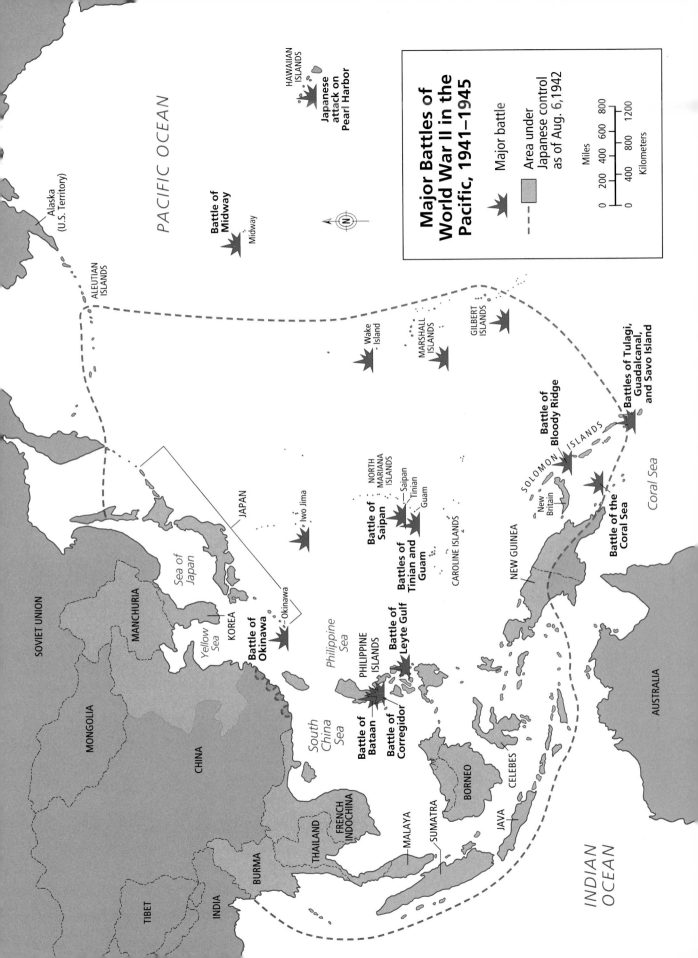

Major Battles of World War II in the Pacific, 1941–1945

Major battle

Area under Japanese control as of Aug. 6, 1942

Miles
0   200   400   600   800

Kilometers
0   400   800   1200

PACIFIC OCEAN

Alaska (U.S. Territory)

ALEUTIAN ISLANDS

HAWAIIAN ISLANDS

Japanese attack on Pearl Harbor

Battle of Midway
Midway

N

Wake Island

MARSHALL ISLANDS

GILBERT ISLANDS

Battles of Tulagi, Guadalcanal, and Savo Island

Battle of Bloody Ridge

SOLOMON ISLANDS

New Britain

Battle of the Coral Sea

Coral Sea

JAPAN

Iwo Jima

NORTH MARIANA ISLANDS

Battle of Saipan
Saipan
Tinian
Guam

Battles of Tinian and Guam

CAROLINE ISLANDS

NEW GUINEA

Sea of Japan

Yellow Sea

KOREA

Okinawa

Battle of Okinawa

Philippine Sea

PHILIPPINE ISLANDS

Battle of Leyte Gulf

Battle of Bataan

Battle of Corregidor

South China Sea

SOVIET UNION

MANCHURIA

MONGOLIA

CHINA

TIBET

INDIA

BURMA

THAILAND

FRENCH INDOCHINA

MALAYA

SUMATRA

BORNEO

CELEBES

JAVA

AUSTRALIA

INDIAN OCEAN

WORLD WAR II IN THE PACIFIC TIMELINE

December 7, 1941	Japan attacks Pearl Harbor, Hawaii.
December 8, 1941	The United States declares war on Japan.
December 8–23, 1941	The Battle for Wake Island takes place.
December 10, 1941	Japan invades Luzon in the Philippines.
December 11, 1941	Germany and Italy declare war on the United States.
March 12, 1942	Under orders from President Roosevelt, General Douglas MacArthur leaves the Philippines.
April 9, 1942	General Jonathan Wainwright surrenders the Philippines.
April 10–24, 1942	Thousands of U.S. and Filipino soldiers endure the Bataan Death March.
April 18, 1942	Doolittle Raiders bomb Tokyo and other Japanese cities.
May 4–8, 1942	The Battle of the Coral Sea is waged.
June 4–7, 1942	The Battle of Midway is fought.
August 7, 1942	Americans invade Tulagi and Guadalcanal, Solomons.
August 9, 1942	The Battle of Savo Island, Solomons, takes place.
September 12–14, 1942	The Battle of Bloody Ridge, Solomons, rages.
November 12–15, 1942	The naval Battle of Guadalcanal is waged.
February 9, 1943	U.S. forces secure Guadalcanal.
November 20–25, 1943	The Battles for Gilbert Islands and Tarawa Atoll are fought.
February 1944	The Battle of the Marshall Islands is waged.
June–July 1944	The Battle of Saipan takes place.
July–August 1944	The Battle of Tinian is fought.
July–August 1944	The Battle of Guam takes place.
October 23–26, 1944	The Battle of Leyte Gulf is waged.
February 19–March 26, 1945	The Battle of Iwo Jima is fought.
April–June 1945	The Battle of Okinawa takes place.
April 12, 1945	President Franklin Delano Roosevelt dies. Harry S. Truman is sworn in as president of the United States.
May 7, 1945	Germany surrenders, ending World War II in Europe.
August 6, 1945	The United States drops an atomic bomb on Hiroshima, Japan.
August 9, 1945	The United States drops an atomic bomb on Nagasaki, Japan.
August 14, 1945	Japan surrenders, ending World War II.
September 2, 1945	Japan signs a surrender agreement aboard the battleship USS *Missouri*.

GLOSSARY

aircraft carrier: a ship with a flat, extra-long deck for launching aircraft

amphibious: able to operate on both land and water

artillery: large cannon that fire explosive shells. Howitzers are a type of artillery.

atoll: a coral island consisting of a reef surrounding a lagoon, or shallow body of water

battleship: the largest class of warship. These ships are protected by heavy armor and armed with big guns.

Bushido: the strict code of samurai warriors, emphasizing loyalty, courage, and self-sacrifice rather than surrender

casualty: a soldier who is killed, injured, captured, or missing in battle

civilian: a person who doesn't belong to the armed services

convoy: a group of ships sailing together for protection

cruiser: a large, fast warship with solid armor and big guns. Cruisers are smaller than battleships.

destroyer: a small, fast warship, usually armed with several five-inch guns and torpedoes

destroyer escort: a warship that is smaller, slower, and less heavily armed than a destroyer. Destroyer escorts sailed with aircraft carriers and other ships, guarding them from enemy submarine attacks.

garrison: an established military base; also the soldiers and officers stationed at such a base

hull: the watertight body of a ship

intelligence: information about an enemy's activities, gathered by spying, intercepting radio messages, surveying enemy territory from airplanes, and other methods

kamikaze: any Japanese pilot who flew a suicide mission, sacrificing himself and his aircraft.

pillbox: a fortified station for machine guns, antitank weapons, and other armaments

propaganda: information and ideas put forth through materials such as films, posters, and magazines, to support a specific cause

radar: a system for detecting objects by means of high-frequency radio waves. The waves bounce off of objects and then return to the radar station, allowing operators to pinpoint the objects' locations.

ration: to distribute food and other goods in limited amounts, in an effort to conserve supplies

salvo: a discharge of similar weapons at or nearly at the same time

shrapnel: fragments of bombs, mines, or shells

strategy: plans and approaches designed to achieve military objectives and victory

tactics: military actions guided by and carried out to fulfill strategies

tourniquet: a tight bandage used to slow or stop severe bleeding

veteran: a soldier with military service, especially combat experience

WHO'S WHO?

James Doolittle (1896–1993)

Born in Alameda, California, Doolittle served as a flight instructor during World War I. Later, he won fame as a test pilot and airplane racer. He graduated from the Massachusetts Institute of Technology in 1925. After his recall into military service in 1940, Doolittle was assigned to lead the famous Doolittle Raid on Japan in April 1942. His plane crash-landed in China, but he eventually returned to the United States, where he received the Medal of Honor for leading the raid.

Mitsuo Fuchida (1902–1976)

One of Japan's best pilots, Fuchida was born in the Japanese city of Kashiwara. In 1941 he was chosen to lead the air attack on the U.S. fleet at Pearl Harbor. Flying at the head of 182 planes, he sent the famous message "Tora, Tora, Tora" ("Tiger, Tiger, Tiger"), to tell his commanders that the attack was a total surprise. He was aboard the flagship *Akagi* when it was sunk at Midway but was rescued from the water. After the war, he converted from his traditional Asian religion to Christianity, became a rice farmer, and eventually moved to the United States, where he became a U.S. citizen.

William Halsey (1882–1959)

Nicknamed "Bull" for his daring and impulsive leadership, Halsey was born in Elizabeth, New Jersey. Graduating from the U.S. Naval Academy in 1904, he commanded destroyers in World War I and later earned a navy pilot's license at age 53. Among the air raids Halsey coordinated was the Doolittle Raid on Japan. In 1945 he became a five-star admiral.

Hirohito (1901–1989)

Japanese emperor Hirohito, born in Tokyo, ascended to the throne at age 25. According to Japanese tradition, emperors were descended from the Shinto sun goddess and were, therefore, divine themselves. Hirohito actually had little say in the government of his country, which was controlled by military leaders. He may have even opposed Japan's military buildup of the 1930s and 1940s. Regardless, it appears that his advisers told him to remain silent about any doubts he might have had about the issue. During the war, Americans viewed Hirohito as a symbol of evil. When the war ended, many Americans felt he should be tried as a war criminal. But as one of the terms of the surrender agreement, he was allowed to remain on the throne as a symbolic ruler (without any actual power).

Oveta Culp Hobby (1905–1995)

Hobby was born in Killeen, Texas. A former attorney in Houston, Texas, she was serving in the public relations bureau of the Department of War when war broke out with Japan. From 1942 to 1945, she was the founding director of the Women's Army Corps, holding the rank of colonel. In 1953 Hobby became the first U.S. secretary of the Department of Health, Education, and Welfare.

Ernest J. King (1878–1956)

Born in Lorain, Ohio, King was responsible for much U.S. naval strategy in World War II. Beginning in March 1942, he was chief of naval operations. In that position, he correctly argued that the United States could fight in Europe and the Pacific at the same time. Known for his foul temper, self-confidence, and brilliant mind, he was frequently at odds with other top commanders, especially General Douglas MacArthur.

Takeo Kurita (1889–1977)

Kurita, who was born in Mito, Japan, commanded the powerful Central Force in the Battle of Leyte Gulf. In his unit were 23 ships, including two superbattleships with 18-inch guns. Opposed to him in the U.S. unit of Taffy 3 were 13 small, slow, and lightly armed vessels. Many historians think his decision to retreat from the fighting was one of the most serious mistakes of the entire Pacific war.

Douglas MacArthur (1880–1964)

Born in Little Rock, Arkansas, MacArthur was the son of General Arthur MacArthur, a famous Civil War hero. He graduated from the U.S. Military Academy at West Point, New York, in 1903, the top student in his class. After a distinguished career in World War I, he was promoted to four-star general at age 50, the youngest man ever to achieve that rank. Brilliant and self-confident, he had difficulty taking orders from men he considered his inferiors. He resisted openly when President Roosevelt ordered him to leave the Philippines in 1942. Later, during the Korean War years, he was so disrespectful to President Harry Truman that the president relieved him of his command (took away his job).

Chuichi Nagumo (1887–1944)

Nagumo was born in the city of Yonezawa, Japan. As commander of the Japanese force that assaulted Pearl Harbor, Nagumo was responsible for a costly mistake. Worried about the security of his attack fleet, he chose to withdraw from the Hawaiian region without bombing U.S. fuel storage and dockyard facilities. A second failure occurred at the Battle of Midway, when he was not notified promptly that U.S aircraft were in the area. As a result, he lost three of his four fleet carriers. Two years later, his 6,800 troops were among the men defeated in the U.S. invasion of Saipan. Nagumo committed suicide on June 6, 1944.

Chester W. Nimitz (1885–1966)

A native of Fredericksburg, Texas, Chester Nimitz graduated from the U.S. Naval Academy in 1905. He took command of the U.S. Pacific Fleet on December 31, 1941, shortly after the attack on Pearl Harbor. He was promoted to fleet admiral in 1944. In this position, Nimitz developed the strategy of island hopping to seize key Pacific islands, from which attacks on other key islands could be launched.

Takijiro Onishi (1891–1945)

Born in Hikami, Japan, Onishi was one of Japan's leading naval pilots. Under Admiral Yamamoto's direction, he planned the Pearl Harbor attack, giving it only a 50-50 chance of success. When the Japanese cause seemed doomed in 1944, he developed the plan for kamikaze attacks on enemy targets, which became a popular tactic throughout the rest of the war. Even after the bombings of Hiroshima and Nagasaki, Onishi opposed surrender. He committed suicide on August 16, 1945.

Ernie Pyle (1900–1945)

Pyle was born near Dana, Indiana. The most famous American war correspondent of World War II, he focused his attention on common soldiers, nicknamed GIs. After reporting from Britain and North Africa, Pyle joined the First Marine Division and waded to shore with the men at Okinawa on April 4, 1945. Two weeks later, he was shot and killed by a Japanese sniper. Burgess Meredith starred in a 1945 movie about Pyle's life called *The Story of GI Joe.*

Jeanette Rankin (1880–1973)

Born near Missoula, Montana, Rankin became the first women ever elected to the U.S. Congress (in 1917, three years before women even had the right to vote). A Republican, she fought for equal pay for women, birth control, trade union rights, and pacifism (the peace movement). After voting against the United States entering World War I, she was defeated in her bid for reelection to Congress. However, she was elected 20 years later and served another term. The day after the attack on Pearl Harbor, Rankin cast the only negative vote for going to war with Japan, a vote that made her extremely unpopular with the American people.

Franklin Delano Roosevelt (1882–1945)

Born in Hyde Park, New York, Roosevelt made politics his career. Elected president of the United States in 1932, he started many programs to bring the nation out of the Great Depression. Despite intense political opposition, he backed U.S. military and industrial preparations for entering World War II. He made alliances with Winston Churchill and Joseph Stalin. His leadership and regular radio addresses inspired the United States to its military and industrial achievements of the war. Roosevelt died in April 1945, before war's end.

Hideki Tojo (1884–1948)

Tojo was born in Tokyo. After commanding the Japanese military police in Manchuria, he served as army chief of staff and prime minister of Japan. To U.S. citizens, Tojo was a symbol of evil and appeared in U.S. cartoons as a short, nearsighted man with a silly moustache. After the fall of Saipan, he was forced to resign as Japan's most important military leader. When U.S. troops came to arrest him in August 1945, he shot himself. However, he recovered from his wounds and lived to stand trial for war crimes. He was convicted and put to death on December 23, 1948.

Harry S. Truman (1884–1972)

Truman was born in Lamar, Missouri, and grew up in Independence, Missouri. During World War I, he commanded an artillery battery in France. After the war, he attended the Kansas City School of Law but never graduated. He went on to become a senator from Missouri, then vice president in 1944. Upon Franklin Roosevelt's death in April 1945, Truman completed Roosevelt's term as president, authorizing the use of the atomic bomb on Japan. In 1948 Truman was elected to a full presidential term.

Alexander A. Vandegrift (1887–1973)

Born in Charlottesville, Virginia, Vandegrift took command of the First Marine Division in April 1942. He was best known for his leadership on Guadalcanal from August to December 1942, which he conducted from makeshift quarters, putting his life in constant danger. That assignment earned him the Medal of Honor, the highest U.S. military award. He also served with distinction in other areas of the Pacific, including Leyte Gulf. Vandegrift was the first marine commandant to earn the rank of four-star general.

Isoroku Yamamoto (1884–1943)

Born in Nagaoka, Japan, Yamamoto attended Harvard University and served as a diplomat in Washington, D.C., in the 1920s. Because of his time in the United States, Yamamoto respected U.S. military strength. Unlike other Japanese leaders, he believed battleships would be phased out of warfare and that Japan should improve its air force. He pushed for a surprise attack against the United States before its factories had time to start making military vehicles and weapons. U.S. leaders regarded Yamamoto as a brilliant and dangerous opponent and set out to kill him. That happened on August 18, 1943, when U.S. fighter pilots shot down his plane over the Pacific Ocean near the island of Bougainville.

SOURCE NOTES

13 "American Experience: The Presidents," *PBS Online,* 2003, <http://www.pbs.org/wgbh/amex/presidents/32-f-roosevelt/psources/ps-pearlharbspeech.html> (March 5, 2004).

13 Gordon Douglass, (memoir, n.d.), n.p.

22 Sam Hanson and Lucille Harten, eds., *The "Good War" in Retrospect: Memories of World War II* (Pocatello, ID: Idaho State University Press, 1987), 84.

27 M. Wayne Silker, in Associated Press, "Wounded Veteran of Two Major Battles Describes Jap Attack." *Rochester Post Bulletin,* March 26, 1943.

31 Lawrence Cracroft, (memoir, n.d.), n.p.

32 Hanson and Harten, 72.

48 Clyde E. Weeks Jr., interview by his son, Richard Weeks.

53 H. Whitney Felt, memoir, 39.

58 Bob Tuft, "Decisive WWII Fight, Gambier Bay's Sinking Recalled." *Houston Chronicle,* November 12, 1994.

60 J. Henry Doscher Jr., *Little Wolf at Leyte Gulf* (Austin, TX: Eakin Press, 1996), back cover.

65 Cracroft, n.p.

66 John Bradley, "Oral History—Iwo Jima Flag Raising," *Naval Historical Center,* 2004, <http://www.history.navy.mil/faqs/faq87-3l.htm> (April 2004).

71 Jeptha J. Carrell, "King One: Service in the United States Marine Corps in World War II" (memoir, n.d.), 16.

74 Margaret Truman, *Harry S. Truman* (New York: William Morrow, 1973), 209.

79 Carrell, 50.

82 J. D. Williams, (papers, Salt Lake City: University of Utah, n.d.), n.p.

83 David McCullough, *Truman* (New York: Simon and Schuster, 1992), 462–463.

SELECTED BIBLIOGRAPHY, FURTHER READING, & WEBSITES

SELECTED BIBLIOGRAPHY

Ambrose, Stephen E. *American Heritage New History of World War II.* New York: Viking, 1997.

Copeland, Robert W. *The Spirit of the "Sammy B."* With Jack E. O'Neill. Ocala, FL: USS *Samuel B. Roberts* Association, 2000.

Doscher, J. Henry, Jr. *Little Wolf at Leyte Gulf.* Austin, TX: Eakin Press, 1996.

Hanson, Sam, and Lucille Harten, eds. *The "Good War" in Retrospect: Memories of World War II.* Pocatello, ID: Idaho State University Press, 1987.

Life magazine, eds. *Our Call to Arms: The Attack on Pearl Harbor.* New York: Time, 2001.

Marrin, Albert. *Victory in the Pacific.* New York: Atheneum, 1983.

Polmar, Norman, and Thomas B. Allen. *World War II: The Encyclopedia of the War Years 1941–1945.* New York: Random House, 1996.

Potter, E. B. *Nimitz.* Norwalk, CT: Easton Press, 1988.

Ross, Bill D. *Iwo Jima: Legacy of Valor.* New York: Vanguard Press, 1985.

Steinberg, Rafael. *Island Fighting, World War II.* Alexandria, VA: Time-Life Books, 1998.

Welsh, Douglas. *The USA in World War 2: The Pacific Theater.* New York: Galahad Books, 1982.

Wheeler, Keith. *The Road to Tokyo.* Alexandria, VA: Time-Life Books, 1979.

Willmott, H. P. *June 1944.* Poole, UK: Blandford Press, 1984.

FURTHER READING

Cutler, Thomas J. *The Battle of Leyte Gulf.* New York: Pocket Books, 1994.

Feifer, George. *Tennozan: The Battle of Okinawa and the Atomic Bomb.* New York: Ticknor and Fields, 1992.

Fremon, David K. *Japanese-American Internment in American History.* Springfield, NJ: Enslow, 1996.

Gaines, Ann Graham. *Douglas MacArthur.* Springfield, NJ: Enslow, 2001.

Goldstein, Margaret J. *World War II—Europe.* Minneapolis: Lerner Publications Company, 2004.

Hinz, Earl. *Pacific Island Battlegrounds of World War II: Then and Now.* Honolulu: Bess Press, 1995.

Josephson, Judith Pinkerton. *Growing up in World War II 1941–1945.* Minneapolis: Lerner Publications Company, 2003.

Lace, William W. *Leaders and Generals.* San Diego: Lucent Books, 2000.

Lazo, Caroline Evenson. *Harry S. Truman.* Minneapolis: Lerner Publications Company, 2003.

Nardo, Don. *World War II in the Pacific.* San Diego: Lucent Books, 2002.

Rice, Earle Jr. *Strategic Battles in the Pacific.* San Diego: Lucent Books, 2000.

Roberts, Jeremy. *Franklin D. Roosevelt.* Minneapolis: Lerner Publications Company, 2003.

Tunnell, Michael O., and George W. Chilcoat. *The Children of Topaz: The Story of a Japanese American Internment Camp.* New York: Holiday House, 1996.

Whitman, Sylvia. *Uncle Sam Wants You! Military Men and Women of World War II.* Minneapolis: Lerner Publications Company, 1993.

———. *V Is for Victory: The American Home Front During World War II.* Minneapolis: Lerner Publications Company, 1993.

WEBSITES

Children of the Camps. A companion to the 2003 PBS documentary of the same name, this site tells the story of Japanese American children who endured internment during World War II. <http://www.pbs.org/childofcamp/index.html>

National Atomic Museum. Developed by the National Atomic Museum, this site offers extensive information on the Manhattan Project, the atomic bomb, and the atomic age. <http://www.atomicmuseum.com>

Naval Historical Center. This site offers visitors a rich photographic and narrative history of the U.S. Navy (the photographic record includes all branches), including information on American wars and operations and eyewitness accounts. <http://www.history.navy.mil/index.html>

The Perilous Fight: America's World War II in Color. Visitors to this site, a companion to the PBS documentary, will learn about World War II battles, the home front, and other aspects of the war. <http://www.pbs.org/perilousfight>

VIDEOS

"Jungle and Ocean." *The Century of Warfare.* DVD. Vol. 5. New York: A&E Home Video, 2003.

"The War at Sea." *The Century of Warfare.* DVD. Vol. 5. New York: A&E Home Video, 2003.

INDEX

ABOUT THE AUTHOR

Barbara Williams is the author of more than 50 books for readers of all ages. Her *Titanic Crossing,* a juvenile novel published two and a half years before the Oscar-winning movie *Titanic* was released, has sold more than one million copies. Williams is married to a retired political science professor and with him has raised four children. She lives in Salt Lake City, Utah.

PHOTO ACKNOWLEDGMENTS

The images in this book are used with the permission of: National Archives, pp. 6–7, 10, 17 (inset), 19, 21, 26, 34, 35, 37, 38, 39, 40, 41, 43, 44 (top), 45, 48, 49, 50, 58, 59, 61, 62, 63, 64, 65, 66, 67, 68, 69, 70, 71, 73, 74, 78 (top), 79, 80, 88 (second from bottom, bottom), 89 (center), 90 (second from bottom, bottom), 91 (top); © CORBIS, pp. 8, 53, 77; Laura Westlund, pp. 11, 14, 17, 60, 75, 85; Independent Picture Service, p. 12; U.S. Naval Historical Center, pp. 18, 20, 22, 24, 28, 29, 30, 31, 32, 51, 52, 56, 88 (top, center), 89 (top, second from top, second from bottom, bottom), 91 (center); U.S. Navy, pp. 25, 91 (bottom); © Hulton Archive/Getty Images, pp. 33, 46; Library of Congress, pp. 36 (LC-USZ62-83890), 78 (bottom; LC-USZ62-20353), 81 (LC-DIG-ppprs-00292), 90 (second from top; LC-USZ62-66358); © Keystone/Getty Images, pp. 42, 88 (second from top); © Museum of Flight/CORBIS, p. 44 (bottom); © Bettmann/CORBIS, pp. 55, 82; Scripps Howard Foundation, p. 90 (top).

Cover: National Archives.